The
Misspeller's Dictionary

The Misspeller's Dictionary

Peter and Craig Norback

Times
BOOKS

This edition is published by TIMES BOOKS, a division of The
New York Times Book Co., Inc., Three Park Avenue, New York,
New York 10016.
  b c d e f g h
1981 EDITION

Manufactured in the United States of America

Library of Congress Cataloging in Publication Data

Norback, Peter G
  The misspeller's dictionary.

  1. Spellers. I. Norback, Craig T., joint author.
II. Title.
PE1146.N7 1980   428'.1   80-26822
ISBN 0-517-33646-4

*Our sincerest thanks to John Hawkins
for helping us with this dictionary.*

Foreword

For years, good spelling has been equated with intelligence, when, in fact, there isn't the remotest relationship between the two. The way one spells most often depends on how one hears sounds or combinations of sounds.

The Misspeller's Dictionary is designed for the thousands of people who spell the way they hear. We began by compiling the most comprehensive list of words that are difficult to spell, and then we misspelled these words. One exception to our rule is that we did not misspell a word if a particular misspelling fell fairly close in alphabetical order to the actual spelling. If you can come that close to the correct spelling, you will be able to find it.

We did, however, misspell extremely difficult words like hemorrhoid (hemroid) because the misspelling very often did not look or sound like the actual word. We did not misspell every word, but we left the difficult words in so that you can check yourself when you get stuck.

The way to use this book is to look up the word you are trying to spell by the way it sounds to you. If the word you are looking up is printed in red type, you have misspelled it. The correct spelling of the word is in black, immediately adjacent to the red word. If the word is in black you have spelled it correctly. All correctly or incorrectly spelled words fall in the alphabetic master list on the left column. To help you with your spelling we have included some basic rules that you should read over and try to keep in mind.

Basic Rules of Spelling

Probably the toughest things to learn in spelling English words are the exceptions. Usually there is quite a list of them following every rule. The best thing to do is to memorize the rules and as many of the exceptions as possible. After awhile you may not remember the specific rule, but you won't forget the problem words.

First Rule
Adding a Suffix to One Syllable Words

Take the word "stop." It's a one syllable word ending in a single consonant (P), and the consonant is preceded by a single vowel (O). When adding a suffix, the last consonant is doubled:

stop + ing = stopping
hot + est = hottest
big + er = bigger

However, the rule does not apply if a word ends with two consonants or if it ends with one consonant preceded by two vowels:

stick + er = sticker
sweet + er = sweeter

Second Rule
Adding a Suffix to a Word with Two or More Syllables

If a word is accented on the last syllable, treat it as if it were a one-syllable word. Double the last consonant if the word ends in a single consonant preceded by a single vowel.

prefer + ing = preferring

Again, the suffix must begin with a vowel.

If the word ends with two consonants or if the final consonant is preceded by two vowels, the rule does not apply.

If the word is not accented on the last syllable, just add the suffix.

The exception is simple. When the accent shifts to the first syllable of the word after the suffix is added, don't double the consonant. A dictionary will help you make the decision here.

Third Rule
Words Ending in a Silent *E*

Usually when the word ends with a silent *e*, drop the *e* if the suffix begins with a vowel:

glide + ing = gliding

Here the exceptions are many.

1. Words with a soft *g* or *c* sound keep the *e* if the suffixes *able* or *ous* are being added.

2. Again, keep the *e* if the word could be mistaken for another word:

dyeing, shoeing

3. If the word ends in *ie*, drop the *e* and change the *i* to *y* before adding *ing*:

dying, lying

4. When adding the suffix *age* to mile, line, acre, the *e* is not dropped.

Fourth Rule
Adding a Suffix with a Consonant to a Word with a Silent *E*

When adding a suffix that begins with a consonant, *ment, ness, less,* and so on, and the word ends with a silent *e*, usually keep the *e*. Some exceptions are judge, true, argue, whole, nine, acknowledge, and awe.

Fifth Rule
The *IE* and *EI*

Almost always use *i* before *e* except after *c*, or when the sound is *a*, like in neighbor and weigh.

The exceptions are:

ancient	neither
foreign	seize
Fahrenheit	sleight
forfeit	sovereign
height	surfeit
leisure	weird

Sixth Rule
Words Ending with *Y*

When a word ends with *y* and is preceded by a consonant, change the *y* to *i* and add the suffix.

Some exceptions are babyhood, beauteous, ladylike, plenteous, and wryly.

If the *y* is preceded by a vowel, there is no change.

A

abace	abase	aberigeny	aborigine
abacus		aberrant	
abait	abate	abet	
abase		abey	abbey
abate		abeyance	
abayance	abeyance	abhor	
abbacus	abacus	abide	
abbé (cleric,		ability	
see abbey)		abismel	abysmal
abberent	aberrant	abiss	abyss
abberigine	aborigine	abject	
abbey (church,		ablate	oblate
see abbé)		abliterate	obliterate
abbreviate		ablivious	oblivious
abbrogate	abrogate	abnormal	
abbrupt	abrupt	A-bomb	
abcense	absence	abominable	
abcent	absent	abomnable	abominable
abcess	abscess	abord	aboard
abdacate	abdicate	abore	abhor
abdamin	abdomen	aborigine	
abdicate		abortion	
abdomen		abragate	abrogate
abdominal		abrasion	
abduct		abreveate	abbreviate
abecus	abacus	abridge	
aberent	aberrant	abrogate	

abrupt	
absalute	absolute
abscence	absence
abscent	absent
abscess	
abscond	
absence	
absent	
absess	abscess
absolute	
absolve	
absorb	
abstain	
abstinence	
abstruse	
absurd	
abuse	
abut	
abysmal	
abyss	
academic	
academy	
a capella	
accalade	accolade
accolite	acolyte
accede (agree, see exceed)	
accelerate	
accent	
accept (receive, see except)	
access (approach, see excess)	
accessory	
accident (miscue,	

see occident)	
acclaim	
acclamation (approval)	
acclimation (adjustment)	
accolade	
accolite	acolyte
accommodate	
accompany	
accomplice	
accomplish	
accord	
accordion	
accost	
account	
accountant	
accredit	
accrete	
accrimonious	acrimonious
accrobat	acrobat
accross	across
accrue	
accumen	acumen
accumulate	
accupuncture	acupuncture
accurate	
accuse	
accustom	
acedemic	academic
acension	ascension
aceptic	aseptic
acetate	
acetic (sour, see ascetic)	

acetone		acrete	accrete
acetylene		acrid	
ache		acrimonious	
achieve		acrobat	
Achilles' tendon		across	
Acilles' tendon	Achilles' tendon	acru	ecru
	acetate	acrue	accrue
acknowledge		acsent	accent
aclaim	acclaim	acsesory	accessory
aclair	éclair	activate	
acne		activities	
acnowledge	acknowledge	actual	
acolade	accolade	actuary	
acolyte		acuity	
acomodate	accommodate	acumalate	accumulate
acompany	accompany	acumen	
acomplice	accomplice	acumulate	accumulate
acomplish	accomplish	acupuncture	
acord	accord	acurate	accurate
acordian	accordion	acuse	accuse
acost	accost	acustics	acoustics
acount	account	acustom	accustom
acountant	accountant	adage	
acoustics		adagio	
acquaint		adamant	
acquaintance		adanoid	adenoid
acquiesce		adapt	
acquire		adaquate	adequate
acquisition		addage	adage
acquit		addament	adament
acquittal		addative	additive
acre		addendum	
acredit	accredit	addenoid	adenoid
		addict	
		additive	

address		adroit	
adduce		aduce	adduce
adegio	adagio	adue	adieu
adelescent	adolescent	adulation	
adelveiss	edelweiss	ad valorem	
adendum	addendum	advantageous	
adenoid		adversary	
adequate		advertisement	
adhere		advice	
adhesive		(suggestion)	
ad hoc		advise	
adict	addict	(give advice)	
adieu (good-bye,		advisable	
see ado)		adviser	
ad infinitum		Aegean	
adjacent		aegis	
adjective		aerate	
adjoining		aerial	
adjourn		aerie (nest,	
adjudicate		see airy)	
adjutant		aerodynamics	
ad-lib		aeronautics	
administer		aerosol	
administrate		aesthetics/	
admirable		esthetics	
admiral		afadavit	affidavit
admissible		afection	affection
ad nauseam		affable	
ado (trouble,		affadavit	affidavit
see adieu)		affect (influence,	
adobe		see effect)	
adnoid	adenoid	affidavit	
adolescent		affiliate	
adopt		affinity	
adrenal		affirmative	

afflict		agrarian		
affluent		agregious	egregious	
afford		agression	aggression	
affray		agriculture		
afghan		agrieved	aggrieved	
afidavit	affidavit	agronomy		
afiliate	affiliate	ahlms	alms	
afinity	affinity	ail (pain, see		
afirm	affirm	ale)		
afirmation	affirmation	air (oxygen,		
aflict	afflict	see err, heir)		
afluent	affluent	airy (open, see		
aforesaid		aerie)		
aforism	aphorism	aisle (passage-		
afraid		way, see I'll,		
afray	affray	isle)		
Afro		ajacent	adjacent	
afrodisiac	aphrodisiac	ajatent	adjutant	
agast	aghast	ajoining	adjoining	
Agean	Aegean	ajourn	adjourn	
agenda		ajudicate	adjudicate	
agglomerate		ajutant	adjutant	
aggrandizement		aknalege	acknowledge	
aggravate		a la carte		
aggregate		alacrity		
aggressive		a la mode		
aggrieved		alamony	alimony	
aghast		alan	elan/élan	
agile		albatross		
agit	agate	albeit		
agitate		albetross	albatross	
agnostic		albino		
agonize		albumen		
agrandizement	aggrandize-	Albuquerque		
	ment	alchemy		

alcohol		alligator	
ale (beer, see ail)		allimentary	alimentary
		allimony	alimony
alegation	allegation	alliteration	
alege	allege	allocate	
aleviate	alleviate	allot (assign, see a lot)	
algae			
alias		allotment	
alibi		allowance	
alien		allowed (per-	
aligarchy	oligarchy	mitted, see	
align/aline		aloud)	
alimentary		alloy	
alimony		allready	already
aline/align		allude (refer to,	
aliteration	alliteration	see elude)	
alkali		all right	
all (the whole, see awl)		allure	
		allusion	
allay (relieve, see alley, ally)		(suggestion, see illusion)	
		alluvial	
allbeit	albeit	ally (friend, see	
alledge	allege	allay, alley)	
allegation		almanac	
allege		almond	
allegiance		almost	
allegory		alms	
allergy		aloha	
alleviate		a lot (many, see allot)	
alley (passage, see allay, ally)			
		alotment	allotment
alliance		aloud (out loud, see allowed)	
allibi	alibi		
allien	alien	alpaca	

alphabet		ambulatory	
already		ameba/amoeba	
alright	all right	ameliorate	
altar (raised		amenable	
place)		amend	
alter (change)		(improve, see	
altercation		emend)	
alter ego		amenity	
alterior	ulterior	amertize	amortize
alternate		amethyst	
although		ametory	amatory
altimeter		amety	amity
altitude		amfedamine	amphetamine
altruism		amfibious	amphibious
alucidate	elucidate	amfitheatre	amphitheater
alum		amiable	
aluminum		amicable	
alumna		amiliorate	ameliorate
alure	allure	amity	
aluvial	alluvial	ammenable	amenable
amalgamate		ammonia	
amateur		ammunition	
amathyst	amethyst	amnesia	
amatory		amnesty	
amaze		amoeba/ameba	
ambassador		amorous	
ambedex-	ambidex-	amorphous	
terous	trous	amortize	
ambidextrous		ampersand	
ambiguity		amphetamine	
ambiguous		amphibian	
ambitious		amphibious	
ambivalence		amphitheater	
ambrosia		amplify	
ambulance		amputate	

amulet

amusement

anachronism

anaconda

analgesic

analogy

analysis

analyze

anarchy

anathema

anatomy

ancellary   ancillary

ancestor

anchor

anchovy

ancient

ancillary

androgen

androsterone

anecdote

anelgesic   analgesic

anemone

anesthesia

anethma   anathema

aneurism

anex   annex

angel (spirit)

angle (geome-
  try/to fish)

angenue   ingenue/
           ingénue

anguish

anicdote   anecdote

anilate   annihilate

animate

animosity

anise

aniversary   anniversary

ankor   anchor

annachronism   anachronism

annaconda   anaconda

annalgesic   analgesic

annals

anneal

annex

annihilate

annimate   animate

anniversary

annoint   anoint

annonymous   anonymous

annotate

announcement

annoy

annual

annuity

annul

annunciation (an-
  nouncement,
  see enunciation)

anode

anoint

anomaly

anonymous

anotate   annotate

anoy   annoy

answer

ansy   antsy

ant (insect, see
  aunt)

antagonize

anteak   antique

antebiotic   antibiotic

antecedence		antiquarian	
antedate		antiquate	
antedote	antidote	antique	
antediluvian		antiquity	
antehistamine	antihistamine	antiroom	anteroom
antelope		anti-semitic	
antenna		antiseptic	
antepasto	antipasto	antisocial	
antequarian	antiquarian	antithesis	
antequate	antiquate	antitoxin	
anteque	antique	antsy	
anteroom		anunciation	annunciation
ante-semetic	anti-semitic	anurism	aneurism
anteseptic	antiseptic	anvil	
antetoxin	antitoxin	anxiety	
anthem		anxious	
anthology		aorta	
anthracite		apaplexy	apoplexy
anthropoid		aparatus	apparatus
anthropology		aparel	apparel
anthropomor-phize		aparent	apparent
		aparition	apparition
antibiotic		apartate	apartheid
antibody		apartheid	
antic		apartite	apartheid
anticedence	antecedence	apartment	
anticipate		apathy	
anticlimax		apeal	appeal
antidate	antedate	apear	appear
antideluvian	antediluvian	apeary	apiary
antidote		apease	appease
antihistamine		apeish	apish
antikuity	antiquity	apellate	appellate
antimacassar		apend	append
antipasto		apendage	appendage
antipathy		apendectomy	appendectomy

apendicitis	appendicitis	apothecary	
apendix	appendix	apothegm	
aperitef	aperitif	apotheosis	
aperitif		appall	
apertain	appertain	apparatus	
aperture		apparel	
apetite	appetite	apparent	
apeture	aperture	apparition	
apex		appartment	apartment
aphorism		appeal	
aphrodisiac		appear	
apierey	apiary	appease	
apiary		appellate	
apitomy	epitome	append	
apish		appendage	
aplaud	applaud	appendectomy	
aplause	applause	appendicitis	
apliance	appliance	appendix	
aplicable	applicable	appertain	
aplicator	applicator	appetite	
aplicatory	applicatory	applaud	
aplied	applied	applause	
aplique	applique	appliance	
aplomb		applicable	
aply	aptly	applicator	
apocalypse		applicatory	
apocryphal		applied	
apointment	appointment	applique	
apoll	appall	apponent	opponent
apology		appointment	
apolstry	upholstery	apportion	
apoplexy		appraise	
aportion	apportion	apprapo	apropos
apostle		appreciate	
apostrophe		apprehend	

apprentice		aquity	acuity
apprise		arabesque	
approach		arable	
approbation		araign	arraign
appropriate		arange	arrange
approval		arangutan	orangutan
approximate		arant	errant (travel-
appurtenance			ing, see
apraise	appraise		arrant)
apreciate	appreciate	aray	array
aprehend	apprehend	arbiter	
aprentice	apprentice	arbitrary	
a preori	a priori	arbitrate	
apricot		arbor	
a priori		arbutus	
aprise	apprise	arc (curve, see	
aproach	approach	ark)	
aprobation	approbation	arcade	
apropos		arcaic	archaic
apropriate	appropriate	arcapelago	archipelago
aproval	approval	arcenal	arsenal
aproximate	approximate	arch	
apruval	approval	archaic	
aptitude		archeology	
aptly		archery	
apurtenance	appurtenance	archetype	
aqua		archipelago	
aquaint	acquaint	architect	
aquaintance	acquaintance	archives	
aquarium		arctic	
aquatic		ardachoke	artichoke
aqueduct		ardent	
aqueous		ardor	
aquiline		arduous	
aquittal	acquittal	arears	arrears

aregano	oregano	arrogate	
aresol	aerosol	arsenal	
argosy		arsenic	
argue		arson	
aria		artacal	article
arial	aerial	artachoke	artichoke
Arian	Aryan	artafac	artifact
arid		artafice	artifice
aristocracy		artaficial	artificial
arithmetic		artasan	artisan
ark (boat, see		arterial	
arc)		arteriosclerosis	
armada		artery	
armadillo		artesian well	
armament		arthritis	
armature		artic	arctic
armistice		artichoke	
armor		article	
arodynamics	aerodynamics	articulate	
arogance	arrogance	artifact	
arogate	arrogate	artifice	
aroma		artificial	
aronautics	aeronautics	artillery	
arora borealis	aurora	artisan	
	borealis	Aryan	
arouse		asail	assail
arpeggio		asassin	assassin
arraign		asatate	acetate
arrange		asault	assault
arrant (bad, see		asay	assay
errant)		asbestos	
array		ascance	askance
arrears		ascend	
arrest		ascension	
arrival		ascent (up, see	
arrogance		assent)	

ascertain		asma	asthma
ascetic (recluse,		asociation	association
see acetic)		asonance	assonance
ascettlin	acetylene	asort	assort
asciduous	assiduous	asparagus	
ascilloscope	oscilloscope	aspursion	aspersion
ascot tie		aspect	
ascribe		aspen	
ascription		asperity	
ascue	askew	aspersion	
asemble	assemble	asphalt	
asembly	assembly	asphyxiate	
asemetry	asymmetry	aspic	
asend	ascend	aspirant	
asent	assent	aspirate	
aseptic		aspire	
asert	assert	aspirin	
asertain	ascertain	assail	
asess	assess	assassin	
aset	asset	assault	
asetic	acetic	assay (analyze,	
asetlin	acetylene	see essay)	
asetone	acetone	assemble	
asetylene	acetylene	assembly	
asfalt	asphalt	assent (agree,	
asfixiate	asphyxiate	see ascent)	
asidious	assiduous	assert	
asign	assign	assess	
asignation	assignation	asset	
asiloscope	oscilloscope	assiduous	
asilum	asylum	assign	
asimilate	assimilate	assignation	
asinine		assimilate	
asistance	assistance	assinine	asinine
askance		assistance	
askew		(help)	

assistants (helper)		atest	attest
association		atheist	
assonance		athlete	
assort		atic	attic
assuage		atire	attire
assume		atitude	attitude
assure		atmosphere	
aster		atoll	
asterisk		atonal	
asteroid		atonement	
asthma		atorney	attorney
astigmatism		atrabute	attribute
astral		atractive	attractive
astringent		atribute	attribute
astrology		atrition	attrition
astronaut		atrocious	
astronomy		atrophy	
astute		attach	
asuage	assuage	attache/attaché	
asume	assume	attack	
asunder		attain	
asure	assure	attainder	
asylum		attar	
asymmetry		attatude	attitude
atach	attach	attempt	
atache	attache	attendance	
atain	attain	attentive	
atainder	attainder	attenuate	
atar	attar	attest	
atavism		attic	
atempt	attempt	attire	
atendance	attendance	attitude	
atentive	attentive	attorney	
atenuate	attenuate	attractive	
		attribute	

attrition
attune
atune   attune
atypical
auburn
auctioneer
audacious
audacity
audible
audience
audio-visual
audit
auditorium
auditory
auger (tool, see
    augur)
aught (small
    part, see
    ought)
augment
au gratin
augur (prophet,
    see auger)
augury
au lait
auld lang syne
au naturel
aunt (relation,
    see ant)
aura
aural (hearing,
    see oral)
aureole (halo,
    see oriole)
aureomycin

au revoir
auricle (outer
    ear, see
    oracle)
aurora borealis
auspices
auspicious
austere
authentic
authoritarian
authorize
autistic
autocracy
automation
automaton
autonomy
autopsy
autumn
auxiliary
avacado   avocado
available
avalanche
avant-garde
avarice
averdupois   avoirdupois
averse
aversion
avert
aviary
aviation
avid
avirdupois   avoirdupois
avocado
avocation
avoirdupois

awareness
away (distant,
  see aweigh)
awe
aweigh (nauti-
  cal, see away)
awful
awkward
awl (tool, see
  all)
awning
awry
axel (skating,
  see axial, axil,
  axle)

axial (forming
  axis, see axel,
  axil, axle)
axil (botany,
  see axel, axial,
  axle)
axiom
axis
axle (shaft, see
  axel, axial,
  axil)
axphyxiate   asphyxiate
aye (yes, see
  eye)
azalea
azure

B

babble
babushka
baccalaureate
bachelor
bacillus
bacteria
bacteriology
badger
badinage
badminton
baffle

bafoon — buffoon

bagatelle

bage — beige

bager — badger

bagetelle — bagatelle

begette — baguette

baggage
baggy
baguette

baige — beige

bail (scoop, see bale)
bailiff

bailiwick

bainful — baneful

bait
   (entice, see
   bate)
bakery
balance
balcony
bale (bundle,
   see bail)

balero — bolero

balestrade — balustrade

balewick — bailiwick

balk

balistic — ballistic

ballad
ballast
ballerina
ballet
ballistic
balloon
ballot
ballyhoo
balm

baloney/boloney (slang, see bologna)		bare (naked, see bear)	
balsa		bargain	
balsam		barge	
balustrade		barister	barrister
bamboo		baritone	
bamboozle		barley	
banal		barnacle	
banana		barometer	
banaster	banister	baron (royalty, see barren)	
bandage		baroque	
bandanna		barracks	
bandeau		barracuda	
banditry		barrage	
bandy		barrecuda	barracuda
baneful		barrel	
banish		barren (sterile, see baron)	
banister		barricade	
bankrupt		barrier	
bankruptcy		barrister	
bannana	banana	barromometer	barometer
banquet		barroom	
banshee		barter	
bantam		basal (base, see basil)	
banter			
baptize			
baracade	barricade	basal metabolism	
baracuda	barracuda		
baratone	baritone	base (foundation, see bass)	
barbarian			
barbecue		baserk	berserk
barber		bases (pl. of base, see basis)	
barbiturate			
barcarole			

bashful
basically
basil (plant, see
  basal)
basilica
basin
basinet (helmet,
  see bassinet)
basis (support,
  see bases)
basket
basmirch   besmirch
bas-relief
bass (music,
  see base)
basset hound
bassinet
  (cradle, see
  basinet)
bassoon
baste
bastille
bastion
batallion   battalion
batch
bate (lessen,
  see bait)
bathe
batiste
baton
battalion
batten
battery
bauble
bauer   bower

bauxite
bawd
bawling
bayonet
bayou
bazaar (market,
  see bizarre)
bazerk   berserk
bazooka
beach (shore,
  see beech)
beacon
beady
beagle
bear (animal,
  see bare)
beast
beastial   bestial
beat (hit, see
  beet)
beau (boy-
  friend, see
  bow)
beautify
beaux-arts
beaver
beckon
becoming
bedaub
bedlam
bedob   bedaub
Bedouin
bedraggled
beech (tree, see
  beach)

beecon	beacon	benaficial	beneficial
Beelzebub		benafit	benefit
beer (drink, see		beneath	
bier)		benediction	
beet (plant, see		benefactor	
beat)		beneficence	
befuddle		beneficial	
beggar		benefit	
begile	beguile	benevolence	
beginning		benidiction	benediction
begonia		benificial	beneficial
begrudge		benifit	benefit
beguile		benign	
behavior		benumb	
behest		Benzedrine	
beholden		benzine	
behoove		bequeath	
beige		bequest	
bekini	bikini	bereave	
belabor		beret	
belatedly		beriberi	
beleaguer		berometer	barometer
belero	bolero	berrage	barrage
belfry		berret	beret
believe		berry (fruit,	
belladonna		see bury)	
beligerent	belligerent	berserk	
bellacose	bellicose	berth (bed, see	
belles-lettres		birth)	
bellicose		berybery	beriberi
belligerent		beseeching	
bellows		besege	besiege
bellwether		beserk	berserk
Belzebub	Beelzebub	besiege	
bemuse		besmirch	

bestial

bestow

betray

betroth

betwixt

bevel

beverage

bevy

bewail

beware

bezerk   berserk

biannial   biennial

biannual

bias

bibliography

bibliophile

bibulous

bicameral

bicarbonate

bicentennial

biceps

bide

biege   beige

biennial

bier (coffin,
    see beer)

bifocal

bigamy

bight (bend,
    see bite)

bigot

bikini

bilateral

bilet   billet

bilinear

bilingual

bilious

billed (invoice,
    see build)

billet

billet-doux

billiards

billious   bilious

billit   billet

billow

bilous   bilious

binary

binaural

bindery

binery   binary

binocular

binoral   binaural

biosynthesis

bipartisan

bipartite

birch

birth (born, see
    berth)

biscuit

biseps   biceps

bison

bisque

bite (cut, see
    bight)

bituminous

bivouac

bivwack   bivouac

bizarre
    (unusual, see
    bazaar)

bladder		blurt	
blarney		boa constrictor	
blase/blasé		boar (pig, see	
blaser	blazer	bore)	
blason	blazon	boarder (guest,	
blasphemy		see border)	
blatant		boast	
blazer		bobalink	bobolink
blazon		bobble	bauble
bleak		bobbin	
bleary		bobolink	
bleat		bochalism	botulism
bleek	bleak	bode	
bleet	bleat	bodice	
blemish		bodlerize	bowdlerize
blert	blurt	bogey (spirit,	
blight		golf)	
blite	blight	boggle	
blithe		bogus	
blitzkrieg		boisenberry	boysenberry
blizzard		boisterous	
bloc (group,		bole (seed, see	
see block)		boll, bowl)	
bloch	blotch	bolero	
block (obstacle,		bolevard	boulevard
see bloc)		boll	
blockade		(tree, see bole,	
blossom		bowl)	
blotch		boll weevil	
blowsy		bologna (meat)	
blubber		boloney/baloney	
bludgeon		(slang)	
blueing/bluing		bolster	
blugeon	bludgeon	bombard	
blunderbuss		bombast	
blurb		bona fide	

bonanza
bondage
bonet   bonnet
boney   bony
bonfire
bonnet
bonny (good,
  see bony)
bonus
bon voyage
bony (of bone,
  see bonny)
booby trap
bookkeeping
boomerang
boondoggle
boorish
booster
bootee (infant's
  sock, see booty)
bootonniere   boutonniere
booty (spoils,
  see bootee)
booze
boquet   bouquet
borax
bordello
border (boun-
  dary, see
  boarder)
bore (puncture,
  see boar)
boric acid
born (birth)
borne (carried)
boron

borough (town,
  see burro,
  burrow)
borrow
borscht
bosom
bossy
botany
botch
botchulism   botulism
botulism
boucle
boudoir
bo weevil   boll weevil
bough (main
  branch, see
  bow)
bouillabaise
bouillon (soup,
  see bullion)
boulder
boulevard
boundary
boundless
bounteous
bouquet
bourbon
bourgeois
boutonniere
bovine
bow (submit,
  see bough)
bow (curve, see
  beau)
bowel
bower

bowery

bowl (dish, see
bole, boll)

boxite   bauxite

boy (male
child, see
buoy)

boycott

boysenberry

bracelet

bracket

brackish

braggadocio

braid

Braille

braise (cook-
ing, see
braze)

brake (stop,
see break)

bramble

brandish

brandy

brasen   brazen

brassiere/
brassière

bravado

bravery

bravo

bravura

brawl

brawny

braze (solder-
ing, see
braise)

brazen

brazier   brassiere/
brassière

breach (break,
see breech)

bread (food,
see bred)

breadth (width,
see breath)

break (destroy,
see brake)

breakfast

breath (respiration,
see breadth)

breathe

breathern   brethren

bred (p.t.,
breed; see
bread)

breech (gun,
see breach)

breeches

breed

breeze

breif   brief

brethren

brevet

breviary

brevit   brevet

brevity

brewery

briar (pipe, see
brier)

bric-a-brac

bricket   briquette

bridal (of a
   wedding, see
   bridle)
bridge
bridle (harness,
   see bridal)
brief
brier (plant, see
   briar)
brig
brigade
brigadier
brigand
brilliance   brillance
brine
brior   briar (pipe)
                              brier (plant)
briquette
brisket
brissle   bristle
bristle
brittle
broach (men-
   tion, see
   brooch)
broad
brocade
broccoli
brochure
brocoli   broccoli
brogue
brokerage
bromide
bronchial
broncobuster

brontosaurus
brooch
   (jewelry, see
   broach)
broshure   brochure
brothel
browbeat
browse
bruise
brunette
brusque
brutal
bubonic plague
buccaneer
buccaroo   buckaroo
buckaroo
bucket
bucolic
budge
budget
buffalo
buffer
buffet
buffoon
bugaboo
bugle
build (construct,
   see billed)
bulevard   boulevard
bullet
bulletin
bullion (gold,
   see bouillon)
bulwark
bumpkin

bumptious
bungalow
bungle
bunion
bunyon   bunion
buoy (float,
  see boy)
bur/burr
burbon   bourbon
burch   birch
burden
bureau
bureaucracy
burette
burgeois   bourgeois
burgeoning
burglar
burial
burlesque
burley
  (tobacco)
burly
  (strong)
burnish
burnt
burr/bur

burro (don-
  key, see
  borough,
  burrow)
burrow (dig,
  see borough,
  burro)
bursar
bury (cover,
  see berry)
bushel
business
bustle
but (con-
  junction,
  see butt)
butcher
butt (ram,
  see but)
butte
buttock/buttocks
button
buttress
burzhwa   bourgeois
buzzard
byfocal   bifocal
byou   bayou

C

cabal

cabaret

cabbage

cabinet

cable

caboose

cache (hiding place, see cash)

cachet

cackle

cacoon   cocoon

cacophony

cactus

cadaver

caddish

cadence

cafeteria

caffeine

cagey

caisson

cajole

calaboose

calamine

calamity

calcedony   chalcedony

calandar   calendar

calcify

calcimine

calcium

calculate

calculous (pathology)

calculus (math)

caldron/cauldron

cale   kale

calendar

calerie   calorie

calesthenics   calisthenics

caliber

calico

caliph

calisthenics

calligraphy

callous (thickened, see callus)

callow

callus (skin, see callous)

calorie		cannibal	
calsify	calcify	cannon (gun,	
calumny		see canon)	
calypso		cannot	
camaflage	camouflage	canny	
camaraderie		canoe	
cameleon	chameleon	canon (church	
camellia		law, see	
cameo		cannon)	
camfer	camphor	canopy (cover,	
camisole		see canapé)	
cammemorate	commemo-	cansel	cancel
	rate	cantaloupe	
camode	commode	cantankerous	
camomile		cantata	
camouflage		canteen	
campaign		canter (talker,	
camphor		see cantor)	
canal		canticle	
canapé (toast,		cantilever	
see canopy)		canto	
canard		canton	
canary		cantor (choir-	
canasta		leader, see	
cancel		canter)	
candescence		canvas	
candidate		(material)	
candle		canvass	
candor		(inquire)	
carnige	carnage	canyon	
canine		caos	chaos
canister		capacious	
canker		caper	
cannery		capillary	

capital (money, seat of government)		cardiogram	
		carisma	charisma
		cardsharp	
capitol (building)		careen	
capitulate		career	
capon		caress	
caprice		caret (printing, see carat, carrot, karat)	
capricious			
capsule			
captain		caribou	
caption		caricature	
captivate		caries (decay, see carries)	
captor			
caracature	caricature	carillon	
caramel		carmel	caramel
carasel	carrousel	carmine	
carat (weight, see caret, carrot, karat)		carnage	
		carnal	
		carnival	
caravan		carnivore	
carberator	carburetor	carode	corrode
carbide		carol (song, see carrel)	
carbine			
carbohydrate		carosion	corrosion
carbon		carousal (drunken revel, see carrousel)	
carbuncle			
carburetor			
carabou	caribou		
carcass		carping	
carcinoma		carrel (a study, see carol)	
cardiac			
cardigan		carriage	
cardinal		carries (transports, see caries)	
carecature	caricature		

carrion		castanet	
carrot (vegetable, see carat, caret, karat)		caste (rank, see cast)	
		caster (stand, see castor)	
carrousel (merry-go-round, see carousal)		castigate	
		castle	
		castor (beaver, see caster)	
cartage		casualty	
carte blanche		catachism	catechism
cartilage		cataclysm	
cartography		catacomb	
carton		catacumen	catechumen
cartoon		catagory	category
cartridge		catalepsy	
casarean	cesarean	catalog/ catalogue	
caserole	casserole		
cascade		catalpa	
casein		catalyst	
cash (money, see cache)		catarpillar	caterpillar
		catapult	
cashew nut		cataract	
cashier		catarrh	
cashmere		catastrophe	
casia	cassia	catatonic	
casino		catechism	
casket		catechumen	
casm	chasm	catecomb	catacomb
cason	caisson	category	
casserole		catelepsy	catalepsy
cassia		catelog	catalog/ catalogue
cassino	casino		
cassock		catelyst	catalyst
cast (throw, see caste)		cater	
		cateract	cataract

cater-corner/
  kitty-corner
caterpillar
catharsis
cathedral
catheter
cathexis
cathode
Catholic
catsup/ketchup
cattalyst   catalyst
catty
catydid   katydid
caucus
caudal (tail)
caudle (drink)
cauldron/caldron
cauliflower
causal
caustic
cauterize
cautious
cavalcade
cavalier
cavalryman
caviar
cavil
cavity
cavort
cease
cedar
cede (grant,
  see seed)
cefalic   cephalic
ceiling
celebrate

celebrity
celerity
celery
celestial
celibate
celuloid   celluloid
cellar (under-
  ground room,
  see seller)
cello
cellophane
cellular
celluloid
cellulose
celophane   cellophane
cement
cemetery
cense (to per-
  fume, see
  cents, scents,
  sense)
censer (vessel,
  see censor)
censor (official,
  see censer)
censure
census (popu-
  lation, see
  senses)
cent (penny,
  see scent,
  sent)
centaur
centenary
centennial
centigrade

centimeter		cesspool	
centrifugal		chafe	
centipetal		chaff	
cents (pl.		chagrin	
pennys, see		chairman	
cense, scents,		chaise longue	
sense)		chalcedony	
centurion		chalee	challis
century (100		chalet	
years, see		chalice	
sentry)		challenge	
cephalic		challis	
cepia	sepia	chamberlain	
ceramics		chambray	
cereal (food,		chameleon	
see serial)		chamfer	
cerebellum		chamise	chemise
cerebral		chamois	
cerebral palsy		champagne	
cerebrum		(wine)	
ceremony		champaign	
cerise		(plan)	
cermudgeon	curmudgeon	chancel	
cerosis	cirrhosis	chancellor	
cerrated	serrated	chancery	
certatude	certitude	chandelier	
certificate		channel	
certify		chantey (song,	
certiorari		see shanty)	
certitude		chanticleer	
cerulean		Chantilly	
cervix		Chanukah/	
cessation		Hanukkah	
cession (yield-		chaos	
ing, see		chaparral	
session)		chapeau	

chapel		cheif	chief
chaperon		chello	cello
chaplain		chemise	
chapter		chenille	
character		cherish	
charade		cheroot	
charcoal		cherub	
charicature	caricature	chervil	
chariot		chevalier	
charisma		chevron	
charivari		chic (stylish,	
charlatan		see sheik)	
charnel		chicanery	
chartreuse		chicano	
charwoman		chickadee	
chary		chicory	
chasee	chassis	chief	
chased (pur-		chiffon	
sued, see		chiffonier	
chaste)		chigger	
chase longe	chaise longue	chignón	
chasm		Chihuahua	
chassis		chime	
chaste (pure,		chimera	
see chased)		chimney	
chastise		chimpanzee	
chastity		chinchilla	
chateau/		chintz	
château		chiropody	
chatelaine		chiropractor	
chattel		chisel	
chatty		chivalry	
chauffeur		chiwawa	Chihuahua
chauvinism		chlorine	
cheetah		chloroform	
chef		chlorophyll	

chocolate

choffeur chauffeur

choir (singers,
 see quire)

choke

cholera

choleric

cholesterol

choral (singers,
 see coral,
 corral)

chord (music,
 see cord)

choreography

chortle

chovinism chauvinism

chrisanthemum chrysanthe-
     mum

christen

chromatic

chrome

chromium

chronic

chronicle

chronological

chronology

chrysalis

chrysanthemum

churlish

chute (slide,
 see shoot)

churvil chervil

Chyanne Cheyenne

cianamide cyanamide

cianide cyanide

cicada

cieling ceiling

cigar

cigarette

cinamon cinnamon

cinch

cinder

cinema

cinic cynic

cinnabar

cinnamon

cintillate scintillate

cipher (code,
 see sypher)

circuit

circular

circumcise

circumference

circumflex

circumlocution

circumscribe

circumspect

circumstance

circumvent

circut circuit

ciropractor chiropractor

cirrhosis

cirriculum curriculum

cirrocumulus

cirrostratus

cirrus

cisegy syzygy

cist (chest,
 see cyst)

cistern

citadel
citation
cite (quote, see
   sight, site)
citology   cytology
civet
civic
civility
clack (noise,
   see claque)
clairvoyance
clammy
clamor
clandestine
clangor
claque
   (applauders,
   see clack)
claret
clarevoyance   clairvoyance
clarify
clarinet
clarion
clarity
classify
clatter
claustrophobia
clavichord
clavicle
cleanse
cleat
cleave
cleche   cliche/
              cliché
clef

cleft palate
clemency
clense   cleanse
cleptomaniac   kleptomaniac
clerical
cliche/cliché
click (sound,
   see clique)
clientele
cliff
climb (ascent)
clime (climate)
clinic
clique (clan,
   see click)
clobber
cloche
cloisonne
cloister
cloraform   chloroform
cloraphyll   chlorophyll
clorine   chlorine
closet
closh   cloche
colesterol   cholesterol
clostraphobia   claustrophobia
closure
cloth
clothe
clothes
clothier
clout
cluster
clutch
coafficient   coefficient

coagulate
coalesce
coalition
coarse (rough,
    see corse,
    course)
coax
cobbler
cobra
cocaine
coccyx
cockatoo
cockleshell
cockney
cocksiks   coccyx
cocoa
cocoon
coddle
co-defendant
codeine
codger
codicil
codify
coefficient
coerce
coessential
coffers
coffin
cofrere   confrere
cogent
coger   codger
cogitate
cognac
cognate
cognition

cognizant
cohere
cohesion
cohort
coiffure
coign (corner,
    see coin,
    quoin)
coin (money,
    see coign,
    quoin)
coincide
coincidence
coition
coitus
colander
colate   collate
colateral   collateral
colembine   columbine
colera   cholera
colesterol   cholesterol
colic
colide   collide
coliflower   cauliflower
coliseum/
    Colosseum
colision   collision
collaborate
collapse
collate
collateral
colleague
collide
collie
colliery

colliflower   cauliflower   commandant
collision   commandeer
colloid   commando
colloquial   commemorate
colloquy   commence
collude   commend
colofon   colophon   commensurate
cologne   commentary
coloid   colloid   commentator
colon   commerce
colonel (officer,   commercial
   see kernel)   commingle
colonnade   commiserate
colony   commissar
colophon   commissary
coloquial   colloquial   commission
coloquy   colloquy   commit
colossal   committee
Colosseum/   commode
   coliseum   commodious
colossus   commodity
colude   collude   commodore
columbine   commondeer   commandeer
column   commotion
collumnar   communal
coma   commune
combat   communicate
comedian   communion
comedienne   communique/
comedy   communiqué
comet   communist
comeuppance   community
comfortable   comuppance   comeuppance
comma   commute
command   comparative

compassionate	comprise	
compatible	compromise	
compel	comptometer	
compelled	comptroller/	
compensate	controller	
compete	compulsion	
competence	compunction	
competition	computer	
competitor	comrade	
complacent	conaseur	connoisseur
(self-satisfied,	conceal	
see complai-	concede	
sant)	conceit	
complain	conceive	
complaisant	concent	consent
(amiable, see	concentrate	
complacent)	concentric	
complement	concept	
(to add, see	concer	concur
compliment)	concern	
complete	concert	
complexion	concertina	
compliant	concerto	
complicate	concession	
complicity	concherto	concerto
compliment	concieve	conceive
(praise, see	conciliate	
complement)	concise	
component	conclude	
compose	concoct	
composite	concomitant	
composition	concord	
compositor	concourse	
comprehend	concrete	
compress	concubine	

concupiscent		congratulate	
concur		congregate	
concussion		congruent	
condement	condiment	conic	
condemn		conifer	
condense		conjagate	conjugate
condenser		conjecture	
condescend		conjest	congest
condiment		conjugal	
condole		conjugate	
condone		conjure	
condor		connect	
conduce		connesseur	connoisseur
conduct		conniption	
conduit		connive	
conefer	conifer	connoisseur	
coneseur	connoisseur	connote	
confer		connubial	
confess		conquer	
confetti		conquistador	
confidant (trusted person)		consanance	consonance
		consanguinity	
confident (self assured)		conscience	
		conscientious	
confiscate		conscious	
conflagration		conscript	
confrere		consecrate	
confuse		consecutive	
conga		consensus	
congeal		consent	
congenial		consequence	
congenital		conservative	
congest		conservatory	
conglomerate		conserve	

consign		contempt
consistent		contend
console		conterminous
consolidate		context
consomme/		contiguous
consommé		continence
consonance		(self-restraint,
conspicuous		see counte-
conspiracy		nance)
conspirator		continent
conspire		contingent
constabulary		continual
constapated	constipated	continuity
constellation		continuum
consternation		contort
constipated		contour
constituency		contraband
constitute		contraception
constrain		contract
constrict		contradict
construe		contralto
consul		contrary
consume		contravene
consummate		contrite
consumme	consomme/	contrive
	consommé	controller/
consumption		comptroller
contact		controversy
contagion		controvert
container		contumacious
contaminate		contusion
contata	cantata	conundrum
contemacious	contuma-	convalescence
	cious	convene
contemplate		convenience
contemporary		converge

converse
conversion
converter
convict
convince
convivial
convocation
convolesence   convalescence
convolution
convulse
conyac   cognac
coo (bill and...,
  see coup)
cookery
coolie
coop (for
  chickens)
co-op (for
  people)
cooperage
cooperate
co-opt
coordinate
copious
copulate
coquette
corador   corridor
coral (sea ani-
  mal, see
  choral, corral)
coranary   coronary
coranation   coronation
cord (string,
  see chord)
cordial
cordisone   cortisone

cordon
cordovan
corduroy
core (center,
  see corps,
  corpse)
corelate   correlate
corener   coroner
corenet   coronet
coreography   chore-
                      ography
corespond   correspond
corespondent
  (adulterer,
  see corre-
  spondent)
corgel   cordial
coriander
cormorant
cornea
cornet (horn, see
  coronet)
cornice
cornucopia
coroborate   corroborate
corode   corrode
corollary
corona
coronary
coronation
coroner
coronet (crown,
  see cornet)
corosion   corrosion
corporal (soldier,
  see corporeal)

corporate

corporeal (physi-
  cal, see corporal)

corps (unit, see
  core, corpse)

corpse (body,
  see core,
  corps)

corpulent

corpuscle

corral (pen,
  see choral,
  coral)

corraner   coroner

correlate

correspond

correspondence
  (letter)

correspondents
  (reporters)

corridor

corroborate

corrode

corrosion

corrupt

corsage

corsair

corset

cortege

corterize   cauterize

cortisone

corupt   corrupt

cosmetic

cosmology

cosmopolitan

cosmos

costic   caustic

costume

cotage   cottage

coterie

cotillion

cottage

cougar

council (meeting)

counsel (advise)

countenance
  (expression,
  see continence)

coup (master-
  stroke, see
  coo)

coup d'etat/
  coup d'état

coupé

coupon

courageous

courier

course (direc-
  tion, see
  coarse)

courteous

courtesan

courtesy

couturier

covenant

covert

covey

coward

cowtow   kowtow

coxix   coccyx

coyote		creosote	
crabby		crepe	
cradential	credential	crescendo	
cradle		crescent	
crag		cresh	creche/
crampon			chèche
cranberry		creshendo	crescendo
cranial		cretin	
cranny		crevasse	
crape	crepe	crevice	
crashe	creche/crechè	cribbage	
cratique	critique	cricket	
cravat		crier	
crayon		criminal	
creak (sound,		crimson	
see creek)		cringe	
creamery		crinkle	
creap	creep	crinoline	
crease		cripple	
creasol	creosol	cript	crypt
creasote	creosote	criptic	cryptic
creature		cripton	krypton
creche/crèche		crisis	
credence		crispy	
credential		cristal	crystal
credible		criterion	
credo		criticism	
credulity		critique	
credulous		croak	
creek (stream,		crochet	
see creak)		crotchety	
creep		crockery	
cremate		crocodile	
creole		crocus	
creosol		croissants	

croft		crusible	crucible
croke	croak	crusifix	crucifix
crokus	crocus	crusify	crucify
cromatic	chromatic	crustacean	
crome	chrome	crutch	
cromium	chromium	crux	
crony		cryer	crier
croquet		crypt	
croquette		cryptic	
crone (old		crypton	krypton
woman, see		crysanthenium	chrysanthe-
krone)			mum
cronic	chronic	crystal	
cronological	chronological	cubical (cube	
crooton	crouton	shaped)	
croshay	crochet	cubicle (en-	
crouch		closure)	
croup		cuboard	cupboard
croupier		cuckold	
crouton		cuckoo	
crovat	cravat	cuddle	
crucial		cudgel	
crucible		cudle	cuddle
crucifix		cue (poolstick,	
crucify		see queue)	
cruel		cugar	cougar
cruet		cugel	cudgel
cruise (voyage,		cuisine	
see cruse)		cul-de-sac	
cruller		culee	coolie
crumble		culinary	
crusade		culminate	
cruse (jar, see		culottes	
cruise)		culpable	
crusial	crucial	cultivate	

cumbersome		curt	
cumin		curtailment	
cum laude		curtain	
cummerbund		curteous	courteous
cumulative		curtesy	courtesy
cumulus		curtsy	
cumquat	kumquat	cushion	
cuneiform		cuspidor	
cunning		cussedness	
cupboard		custard	
cupidity		custody	
cupola		customary	
cupon	coupon	cutaneous	
curacao/		cuticle	
curaçao		cutlass	
curate		cutlery	
curator		cuturier	couturier
curdle		cyanamide	
curette		cyanide	
curfew		cycle	
curiculum	curriculum	cycletron	cyclotron
curier	courier	cycloid	
curious		cyclometer	
curlicue		cyclone	
curmudgeon		cyclopedia	
currant (berry,		cynch	cinch
see current)		cyclotron	
currate	curate	cygnet (swan,	
currator	curator	see signet)	
current		cylinder	
(present, see		cymbal (music,	
currant)		see symbol)	
curriculum		cynic	
curry		cyote	coyote
cursory		cypher	cipher

cypress   cystalic   systalic
cysegy   syzygy   cytology
cyst (growth,   czar/tsar
  see cist)

D

dabble		damn (con-	
dabut	debut	demn, see	
Dachshund		dam)	
dacollete	decollete/	damsel	
	décolleté	dandelion	
dacor	decor/décor	dandruff	
Dacron		dane	deign
daffodil		dangle	
dagerotype	daguerreo-	danoman	denouement
	type	dapper	
dagger		daring	
daguerreotype		dashboard	
dahlia		dastardly	
dainty		daub	
dairy (milk		dauntless	
farm, see		dauphin	
diary)		dawdle	
daisy		daze	
dakshund	Dachshund	dazzle	
dalia	dahlia	deacon	
dally		deaf	
dam (block,		deam	deem
see damn)		dearth	
damage		debacle	
damask		debasement	

debauch		declivity	
debenture		decollete/	
debetor	debtor	décolleté	
debilitate		decompose	
debit		decon	deacon
deboch	debauch	decontaminate	
debonair		decor/décor	
debris		decorate	
debtor		decorous	
debunk		decorum	
debut		decrepit	
decadence		dedicate	
decal		deduce	
decanter		deem	
decapitate		defecate	
decathlon		defenite	definite
deceased		defense	
decedence	decadence	defer	
deceit		deference	
deceive		deferential	
decelerate		deffuse	diffuse
decent		defiance	
deception		deficiency	
decerous	decorous	deficit	
decibel		definite	
decide		definitive	
deciduous		deflower	
decieve	deceive	defray	
decimal		deft	
decimate		defunct	
decipher		defy	
decision		degenerate	
decisive		dehumidify	
declamation		dehydrate	
declension		deify	

deign		demise	
deity		demitasse	
delapidated	dilapidated	demiurge	
delectable		demobilize	
delegate		democracy	
delemma	dilemma	demolish	
deleterious		demonetize	
deliberate		demonstrate	
delicate		demoralize	
delicious		demur (objec-	
delineate		tion)	
delinquency		demure (re-	
delinquent		served)	
delirious		dendrite	
delirium		denem	denim
delude		denigrate	
deluge		denim	
delute	dilute	denizen	
deluxe		denominator	
demagnetize		denouement/	
demagogue		dénouement	
deman	demesne	dense	
demask	damask	denunciate	
demean		deodorant	
demeanor		deoxidize	
demension	dimension	depaty	deputy
dementia		dependent	
precox		depict	
demerit		depilatory	
demeurge	demiurge	deplete	
demesne		depolarize	
demilitarize		depopulate	
deminish	diminish	deportation	
deminution	diminution	deposition	
deminutive	diminutive	depository	

depot		desel	diesel
depravation		desend	descend
(corruption,		desendant	descendant
see depriva-		desensitize	
tion)		desert (arid,	
deprecate		see dessert)	
depreciate		desible	decible
depredation		desiccate	
depressant		desicrate	desecrate
depression		desideratum	
deprivation		design	
(loss, see		designate	
depravation)		desirable	
deputy		desist	
derelict		desolate	
derick	derrick	Desopxyn	
dering-do	derring-do	despair	
derivation		desparage	disparage
dermatology		desperado	
derogate		desperate	
derogatory		despicable	
derrick		despise	
derring-do		despite	
derrogate	derogate	despondence	
derth	dearth	despot	
dervish		dessert (food,	
descant		see desert)	
descend		destination	
descendant		destine	
descern	discern	destiny	
desciple	disciple	destitute	
describe		destroy	
desease	disease	destruction	
desecrate		desuetude	
desegregate		desultory	

detach		dewy	
detail		Dexedrine	
detain		dexterity	
deter		dextrose	
deterent	deterrent	diabetes	
detergent		diabolic	
deteriorate		diacese	diocese
determine		diadem	
deterrent		diafanous	diaphanous
dethrone		diafragm	diaphragm
detonate		diagnose	
detor	debtor	diagnosis	
detour		diagonal	
detract		diagraming	
detriment		dial	
deuce		dialect	
devaluate		dialogue	
devastate		diameter	
develop		diametric	
deviate		diamond	
device (invention,		diaper	
see devise)		diaphanous	
devide	divide	diaphragm	
devine	divine	diarrhea	
devinity	divinity	diary (record,	
devisible	divisible	see dairy)	
devisor	divisor	diathermy	
devorce	divorce	diatribe	
devious		dice	
devise (plan,		dichotomy	
see device)		dickey	
devitalize		dictate	
devolve		dictionary	
devour		dictum	
devout		didactic	

die (death, see
  dye)
diedem   diadem
diesel
differ
difference
differential
differentiate
difficult
diffidence
diffract
diffuse
digestible
digit
digital
digitalis
dignify
dignitary
dignity
digress
dilapidated
dilatante   dilettante
dilate
dilatory
dilemma
dilettante
diligence
dilicious   delicious
dillydally
dilute
dimension
diminish
diminution
diminutive
dimity
dinasaur   dinosaur

diner (restaurant,
  see dinner)
dinette
dinghy
dinner (meal,
  see diner)
dinosaur
diocese
diorama
dioxide
diper   diaper
diphtheria
diphthong
diploma
diplomacy
dipper
dipsomania
diptheria   diphtheria
dipthong   diphthong
directorate
directory
dirge
dirigible
dirndl
dirth   dearth
disability
disabille   dishabille
disaffection
disaffirm
disallow
disappear
disappoint
disapprobation
disapprove
disarmament
disarming

disarrange
disarray
disassemble
disassociate
disaster
disastrous
disavow
disbelieve
disburse
disc/disk
discard
disceminate   disseminate
discern
discernible
discheveled   disheveled
discidence   dissidence
disciple
disciplinary
discipline
disclaimer
discomfit
discomfort
discomposure
disconcerting
disconnect
disconsolate
discontinue
discordant
discourage
discourse
discourteous
discoverable
discovery
discreditable
discreet (tactful,
   see discrete)

discrepancy
discrete (distinct,
   see discreet)
discretion
discribe   describe
discriminate
discursive
discurteous   discourteous
discus (disk)
discuss (talk)
discussion
disdain
disect   dissect
disease
disembark
disembody
disembowel
disenchant
disencumber
disenfranchise
disengage
disension   dissension
disentanglement
disentery   dysentery
disesteem
disfunction   dysfunction
disgorge
disgruntled
disguise
disgusting
dishabille
disharmony
dishearten
disheveled
dishonesty
disillusion

disinclined		disrupt
disinfect		dissanance dissonance
disingenuous		dissapate dissipate
disinherit		dissatisfy
disintegrate		dissect
disinter		dissemble
disk/disc		disseminate
dismal		dissension
dismantle		dissent
dismiss		dissentient
disobedience		dissern discern
disobey		dissertation
disobliging		disservice
disoriented		dissheveled disheveled
dispair despair		dissidence
disparage		dissimilar
disparate		dissimilate
dispassionate		(unlike)
dispatch		dissimulate
dispel		(conceal)
dispensable		dissipate
dispensary		dissociate
dispenser		dissolute
dispepsia dyspepsia		dissolution
disperse		dissolve
dispicable despicable		dissonance
dispirited		dissuade
dispise despise		dissymmetry
dispite despite		distaff
displease		distance
dispose		distemper
dispossess		distinct
disproportion		distinguished
disregard		distort
disrepair		distortion
disrepute		distract

distrait
distraught
distribution
distrophie   dystrophy
disturbance
ditty
diurnal
divan
diverge
divers
diverse
divide
dividend
divine
divinity
divisible
division
divisor
divorce
divot
divulge
divurge
divvy
Doberman
  pinscher
docia   dossier
docile
docket
document
doddering
dodge
doggerel
dogma
doily
doldrums
doleful

dollop
dolly
dolorous
dolphin
doltish
domain
domicile
dominant
domineer
dominion
domino
donate
donkey
donor
donut   doughnut
doodle
dormant
dormitory
dormouse
dorsal
dory
dosage
dosea   dossier
doshund   dachshund
dossier
dote
douche
doughnut
dour
douse
dowager
dowdy
dowel
dower
dowry
doxology

doze
drachma
draft/draught
dragon
drapery
draught/draft
drawl
drawn
drayage
dreary
dredge
dribble
driblet
drivel
drizzle
droll
dromedary
drone
droopy
dropsy
drought/drouth
drowsy
drudge
druid
drunkard
drunkenness
dual (two, see
  duel)
dubious
ducal
ducat
duce   deuce
duche   douche
duchess

duchy
ductile
dudgeon
duel (contest,
  see dual)
duet
duffel bag
duffer
dukedom
dulcet
dulcimer
dumbbell
dumfound
dungaree
dungeon
duodenum
duplicate
duplicity
durable
duration
duress
durndl   dirndl
dwarf
dwindle
dye (coloring,
  see die)
dynamic
dynamite
dynamo
dynasty
dysentery
dysfunction
dyspepsia
dystrophy

E

eager		ecstatic	
eagle		ectoderm	
eak	eke	ectomorph	
easel		ectoplasm	
eavesdrop		ecumenical	
ebet	abet	eczema	
ebony		eddy	
ebullient		edefication	edification
eccentric		edefice	edifice
ecclesiastical		edefy	edify
eccumenical	ecumenical	edelweiss	
echelon		edgy	
echo		edible	
eclair		edict	
eclectic		edification	
eclesiastical	ecclesiastical	edifice	
eclipse		edify	
eclogue		Edipus	Oedipus
ecology		edition	
ecologist		editor	
economic		editorial	
economy		education	
ecru		educator	
ecsentric	eccentric	educe	
ecstasy		edy	eddy

eek	eke	eighteen	
eerie		eighth	
efedrine	ephedrine	eightieth	
efemeral	ephemeral	eighty	
efeminate	effeminate	eire	eyre
efervescence	effervescence	either	
efete	effete	ejaculate	
efface		eject	
effect (conclu-		eke	
sion, see affect)		elaborate	
effectual		elagiac	elegiac
effeminate		elagize	elegize
effervescence		elagy	elegy
effete		elament	element
efficacious		elamental	elemental
efficacy		elamentary	elementary
efficient		elamosynary	eleemosynary
effigy		elan/élan	
effort		elaphant	elephant
effrontery		elaphantine	elephantine
effusion		elapse	
effusive		elastic	
eficacy	efficacy	elate	
eficient	efficient	elation	
egalitarian		elavate	elevate
ego		elavation	elevation
egocentric		elavator	elevator
egoism		elbow	
egotism		elderberry	
egotistical		elderly	
egregious		electoral	
egress		electorate	
egret		electric	
eguana	iguana	electrocardiogram	
eider down		electrocute	

electrode		elipsis	ellipsis
electrodynamics		elision	
electrolysis		elite	
electrolytic		elixir	
electromagnetic		ellipse	
electron		ellipsis	
electronic		elocution	
electroplate		elongate	
electrotherapy		elope	
eleemosynary		eloquence	
elegance		elucidate	
elegible	eligible	elude (avoid,	
elegibility	eligibility	see allude)	
elegiac		elusion (escape,	
elegize		see illusion)	
elegy		elusive	
element		emaciate	
elemental		emaciation	
elementary		emanate	
elephant		emanation	
elephantine		emancipate	
elequence	eloquence	emasculate	
elete	elite	embalm	
elevate		embankment	
elevation		embargo	
elevator		embark	
eleven		embarkation	
elfin		embarrass	
elicit (evoke,		embassy	
see illicit)		embattle	
elide		embed	
eligibility		embellish	
eligible		ember	
eliminate		embezzlement	
elipse	ellipse	embilical cord	umbilical cord

embitter   emissary
emblazon   emission
emblem   emit
emblematic   emollient
embody   emolument
embolden   emotion
emboss   empathy
embrace   Emperin   Empirin
embroider   empetigo   impetigo
embroidery   emperor
embroil   emphasis
embryo   emphasize
embryology   emphatic
embryonic   empire
emcee/M.C.   empirean   empyrean
emegra   emigre/émigré   empiric
emend (change,   empirical
   see amend)   empiricism
emerald   Empirin
emerge   emplacement
emergency   employ
emeritus   employable
emersion (coming   employe/
   forth, see   employee
   immersion)   emporium
emery   empower
emetic   empresario   impresario
emigrant   empyrean
emigrate (place   emulate
   to place, see   emulsify
   immigrate)   emulsion
emigration   enable
emigre/émigré   enactment
eminent (promi-   enamel
   nent, see imma-   enamored
   nent, imminent)   encampment

encephalitis
encephalogram
enchant
encircle
enclasp
enclave
enclose/inclose
enclosure
encomium
encompass
encore
encounter
encourage
encroach
encrust
encumber
encumbrance
encyclical
encyclopedia
encyst
endanger
endear
endeavor
endemic
endive
endocrine
endocrinology
endorse
endowment
endue/indue
endurance
endure
enebriate   inebriate
enema
enemy
energetic

energize
energy
enervate (sap
    vitality, see
    innervate)
enfeeble
enforce
enfranchise
engage
engender
English
engine
engineer
engrave
engross
engulf
enhance
enharmonic
enigma
enigmatic
enjoin
enlightenment
enlist
enliven
en masse
enmesh/inmesh
enmity
ennoble
ennui
enormous
enormity
enomaly   anomaly
enough
enplane
enrage
enrapture

enrich		entry
enroll		entwine
en route		enumerate
ensconce		enunciate
ensemble		enunciation (pro-
enshrine		nunciation, see
enshroud		annunciation)
ensign		envelop (enclose)
enslave		envelope
ensue		(wrapper)
entail		envelopment
entangle		envenom
enterprise		enviable
entertain		envious
enth degree	nth degree	environment
enthrall		environmental
enthrone		environs
enthusiasm		envisage
enthusiast		envision
enthusiastic		envoy
entice		envy
entirely		enwrap
entirety		enzyme
entitle		eon
entity		epathet	epithet
entomology		epaulet
entourage		epetaph	epitaph
entrails		ephedrine
entrance		ephemeral
entrant		Epifany	Epiphany
entreat		epic
entree		epicure
entrenchment		epicurean
entrepreneur		epidemic
entrust		epidermis

epigram		equivocate	
epigrammatic		era	
epilepsy		eradicate	
epileptic		eradicator	
epilogue		erand	errand
Epiphany		erant	errant
Episcopalian		erase	
episode		eraser	
epistle		erasure	
epitaph		erate	aerate
epithet		eratic	erratic
epitome		eratum	erratum
epitomize		erb	herb
epoch		erect	
epochal		erecter	
epprobrious	opprobrious	erection	
equable		ergo	
equal		erie	eerie
equalize		ermine	
equanimity		erode	
equate		eroneous	erroneous
equator		erosion	
equatorial		erotic	
equestrian		err (mistake, see	
equidistant		air, heir)	
equilateral		errand	
equilibrium		errant (traveling,	
equine		see arrant)	
equinoctial		erratic	
equinox		erratum	
equip		erroneous	
equitable		error	
equity		ersatz	
equivalent		erstwhile	
equivocal		erudite	

erupt		essential	
Eryan	Aryan	establish	
escalate		estate	
esay	essay	esteem	
escalator		esthetics/	
escapade		aesthetics	
escape		estimable	
escarole		estimate	
escarp		estop	
eschew		estoppage	
escort		estrange	
escrow		estrogen	
escue	eschew	estrus (or	
Esculous	Aeschylus	oestrus)	
escutcheon		estuary	
esel	easel	estute	astute
esence	essence	et cetera	
esential	essential	etching	
eshelon	echelon	eternal	
esop	Aesop	eternity	
esophagus		ether	
esoteric		ethereal	
Espagnole		ethical	
especially		ethics	
Esperanto		ethnic	
espionage		ethnocentrism	
esplanade		ethos	
espouse		ethyl	
espresso		etible	edible
esprit de corps		etiology	
espy		etiquette	
esquire		Etruscan	
essay (try, see		etude	
assay)		etymology	
essence		eucalyptus	

Eucharist	exact	
euchre	exaggerate	
eugenic	exalt (glorify,	
eulogy	see exult)	
eulogize	examine	
eunuch	examination	
euphemism	example	
euphonic	exasperate	
euphoria	excavate	
eureka	exceed (outdo,	
Eustachian tube	see accede)	
euthanasia	excel	
evacuate	excellent	
evade	excellerate	accelerate
evaluate	excelsior	
evanescent	excentric	eccentric
evangelical	except (exclude,	
evangelist	see accept)	
evaporate	excerpt	
evasion	excess (overage,	
eventide	see access)	
eventual	exchequer	
eventually	excise	
evesdrop eavesdrop	excite	
evict	exclaim	
evidence	exclamation	
evidently	exclamatory	
evince	exclude	
eviscerate	exclusive	
evocation	excommunicate	
evocative	excoriate	
evoke	excrement	
evolution	excrescence	
evolve	excrete	
exacerbate	excretory	

excruciating
excursion
excusable
excuse
execrable
execute
executive
executrix
exegesis
exemplary
exemplify
exempt
exercise (activity,
   see (exorcise)
exert
exhalation
exhale
exhaust
exhibit
exhibitor
exhilarate
exhort
exhortation
exhume
exigency
exiguous
exile
exist
existence
existentialism
exodus
exonerate
exorable
exorbitant

exorcise (expell
   spirits, see
   exercise)
exotic
expand
expanse
expatriate
expectant
expectorate
expedient
expedite
expedition
expeditious
expel
expendable
expenditure
expense
experience
experiment
expert
expertise
expiate
expiration
explain
explanatory
expletive
explicable
explicatory
explicit
exploit
explore
explosion
exponent
export

expose
expose/exposé
exposition
ex post facto
expostulate
exposure
expound
express
expropriate
expulsion
expunge
expurgate
exquisite
extant (lasting,
  see extent)
extasy   ecstasy
extatic   ecstatic
extemporaneous
extemporize
extension
extensive
extent (size, see
  extant)
extenuate
exterior
exterminate
external
extinct
extinguish
extirpate
extol
extort

extract
extracurricular
extradite
extramarital
extraneous
extraordinary
extrapolate
extrasensory
  perception
extraterritorial
extravagance
extreme
extremist
extricable
extricate
extrinsic
extrovert
extrusion
exuberant
exude
exult (jubilant,
  see exalt)
exultation
exume   exhume
exzema   eczema
eye (vision,
  see aye)
eyelet (hole,
  see islet)
eyre (journey,
  see ire)

F

fabricate

fabulous

facade

facet

facetious

facile

facility

facsimile

faction

factory

factorum

factsimile   facsimile

factual

faculty

faddist

Fahrenheit

failure

faint (pass out,
   see feint)

fairy (pixie, see
   ferry)

fait accompli

faker (one who
   fakes)

fakir (Hindu

falable   fallible

falacious   fallacious

falanx   phalanx

falcon

fallacious

fallacy

fallible

fallic   phallic

Fallopian tube

fallow

fallus   phallus

Falopian tube   Fallopian tube

falow   fallow

falsetto

falsify

falsity

falter

familiar

family

famine

famish

famous

fanagle   finagle

fanatic

fandango

fanfare

fantastic
fantasy
fantom   phantom
farce
farina
Farisee   Pharisee
farther (more dis-
    tant, see
    further)
farynx   pharynx
fasade   facade
fascetious   facetious
fascinate
fascism
faset   facet
fasilitate   facilitate
fasility   facility
fasle   facile
fasten
fastidious
fatal
fathom
fatigue
fatten
fatuous
faucet
fault
faun (deity, see
    fawn)
fauna
faux pas
favorite
fawn (deer, see
    faun)
faze (disturb,
    see phase)

feable   feeble
feance   fiance/fiancé
                              (male)
                          fiancee/fianceé
                              (female)
                          pheasant
                          fiasco
feasible
feat (deed, see
    feet)
feather
feckless
fecund
fedelity   fidelity
fedora
feduciary   fiduciary
feeble
feet (pl. foot,
    see feat)
feign
feind   fiend
feirce   fierce
feint (trick,
    see faint)
felicitate
felicity
feline
felon
felony
feminine
femme fatale
fennel
fenobarbital   phenobarbital
fenomenon   phenomenon
fenotype   phenotype
feord   fjord

feott	fiat	fiddle	
feral		fidelity	
fer-de-lance		fidget	
ferlough	furlough	fiduciary	
ferment		fiend	
ferocious		fierce	
ferret		fiery	
ferrous		fiesta	
ferry (boat, see		fifth	
fairy)		fiftieth	
fertile		fifty	
fertilize		figet	fidget
fervent		figment	
fervid		figurine	
fervor		filabuster	filibuster
festival		filament	
festoon		filanderer	philanderer
fether	feather	filately	philately
fetid		filbert	
fetish		filch	
fetter		fileal	filial
fetus		filegree	filigree
feud		filial	
feudal (medieval,		filibuster	
see futile)		filigree	
fever		Filipino	
fiance/fiancé		fillament	filament
(male)		fillet	
fiancee/fianceé		filly	
(female)		filodendron	philodendron
fiasco		filogeny	phylogeny
fiat		filtch	filch
fibrillation		filter (strainer,	
fickle		see philter)	
fictitious		filthy	

finacky	finicky	flamboyant	
finagle		flamenco	
finale		flamingo	
finance		flammable	
financier		flapper	
finesse (trick,		flare (blaze, see	
see finis)		flair)	
finicky		flattery	
finis (end, see		flaunt	
finesse)		flavor	
finish		flaxen	
finite		flea (insect, see	
finnig	phennig	flee)	
fiord/fjord		fledgling	
fir (tree, see fur)		flee (run away,	
firmament		see flea)	
fiscal (finance,		fleece	
see physical)		flegmatic	phlegmatic
fission		flem	phlegm
fissure		fleur-de-lis	
fistic		flew (did fly,	
fisticuffs		see flu, flue)	
fixation		flexible	
fizzle		flimsy	
fjord/fiord		flippant	
flabbergast		flirtation	
flaccid		floage	flowage
flack	flak	flocculate	
flagellate		flogistic	phlogistic
flagon		flogging	
flagrant		floral	
flair (insight,		florescent	fluorescent
see flare)		floriculture	
flak		florid	
flamable	flammable	floridate	fluoridate

florinate	fluorinate	Foebe	Phoebe
floroscope	fluoroscope	fogy (person,	
flotation		see foggy)	
flotilla		foggy (weather,	
flotsam		see fogy)	
flounce		foible	
flounder		foier	foyer
flour (grain, see		foist	
flower)		folcrum	fulcrum
flowage		foleage	foliage
flower (blossom,		foliage	
see flour)		folio	
flu (influenza,		follicle	
see flew, flue)		folly	
fluctuate		folsetto	falsetto
flue (chimney,		foment	
see flew, flu)		fon	faun
fluent		fona	fauna
flugel horn/		fondant	
flügel horn		fondle	
fluid		fondue	
fluke		fonetic	phonetic
flummox		fo pa	faux pas
fluorescent		foppery	
fluoridate		forage	
fluorinate		foray	
fluoroscope		forceps	
flur-de-lee	fleur-de-lis	forcible	
flurry		forebear	
flute		foreclosure	
flutter		foreign	
fobia	phobia	forensic	
fobic	phobic	foreword	
focal		(preface, see	
focus		forward)	
fodder		forego	forgo

forfeit

forge

forgery

forgo

forlorn

formaldehyde

formally (cus-
    tom, see
    formerly)

format

formative

formerly (past,
    see formally)

formidable

formula

forrensic   forensic

fosphate   phosphate

fosphorescense   phosphor-
                    escence

forsythia

fort (stronghold)

forte (ability)

forth (forward,
    see fourth)

fortieth

fortify

fortissimo

fortitude

fortnight

fortress

fortuitous

fortunate

forty

forum

forward (near,
    see foreword)

fossil

foto   photo

foul (ugly, see
    fowl)

foundation

foundry

fountain

fourteen

fourth (after
    third, see
    forth)

fowl (bird, see
    foul)

foyer

fracas

fraction

fracture

fragile

fragment

fragrant

fraight   freight

frail

franchise

frankfurter

frankincense

frantic

frantically

frappe/frappé

fraternity

frau

fraud

fraught

fraulein/
    fraülein

freakish

freedom

freeze (cold,
  see frieze)
frehol   frijole
freight
frenetic/phrenetic
frenology   phrenology
frenzy
frequent
fresco
Freudian
freülein   fraulein/
                 fraülein
friar (clergy, see
  fryer)
fricassee
friend
frieze (orna-
  ment, see
  freeze)
frigate
frigid
frijole
fringe
frippery
frisky
fritter
frivolous
frolic
frontier
frontispiece
frothy
frugal
fruition
frustrate
fryer (chicken,
  see friar)

fuchsia
fudal   feudal
fude   feud
fuehrer
fugitive
fugue
fulcrum
fulfill
fulsome
fumigate
fundamental
funeral
funeral (service)
funereal (sad)
funnel
fur (animal skin,
  see fir)
furl
furlough
furnace
furer   fuehrer
furniture
furor
furrow
further (in addi-
  tion, see
  farther)
furtive
fuse
fuselage
fushia   fuchsia
fusible
fusillade
futile (useless,
  see feudal)
futurity

G

gabardine (coat)
gaberdine
  (fabric)
gadfly
gadget
gage (pledge, see
  gauge)
gaget   gadget
gaiety/gayety
gait (way of
  walking, see
  gate)
galaxy
Galic   Gaelic
gallant
galleon
gallery
galley
gallop
galore
galosh
galvanize
gama   gamma
gambit
gamble (to bet)
gambol (play)

gamma
gamut
gangling
ganglion
gangrene
garage
garbage
gard   guard
gardenia
gardian   guardian
garelous   garrulous
gargantuan
gargoyle
garish
garlic
garnishee
garrison
garrulous
gaseous
gasket
gastly   ghastly
gastric
gastronomy
gate (opening,
  see gait)
gauche

gaudy
gauge (measure,
   see gage)
gaunt
gauntlet
gauze
gavel
gawk
gayety/gaiety
gazebo
gazelle
gazette
Geiger counter
geiser   geyser
geisha
gelatin
gendarme
gene (heredity,
   see jean)
geneal   genial
genealogy
generate
generic
generous
genesis
genetics
genial
genital
genitive
genius
genocide
genre
genteel
gentian
gentile
gentility

gentleman
gentry
genuflect
genuine
genus
geodesic
geodetic
geography
geology
geometry
geophysics
geopolitical
geraffe   giraffe
geranium
gerend   gerund
gergle   gurgle
geriatrics
gerkin   gherkin
germane
germicide
germinal
germination
gerrymander
Gerter   Goethe
gerund
gesha   geisha
gest/geste
   (adventure,
   see jest)
gestation
gesticulate
gesture
gesundheit
geyser
ghastly
gherkin

ghetto		gizzard	
ghoulish		glacier	
giant		gladiator	
gibberish		gladiola	
gibbon		glamour	
gibe/jibe		glandular	
giblet		glib	
gigantic		glicerin	glycerin
giger counter	Geiger counter	glimmer	
gigolo		glimpse	
gila monster		glisten	
gild (gold covered, see guild)		gloat	
		global	
		globular	
gile	guile	gloomy	
gillotine	guillotine	glorify	
gilt (gold-colored, see guilt)		glorious	
		glossary	
		glossy	
gimmick		glote	gloat
gingham		glucose	
gingivitis		glutton	
ginny pig	guinea pig	glycerin	
ginocology	gynecology	gnarl	
ginrikisha	jinrikisha	gnash	
gip	gyp	gnat	
gipsum	gypsum	gnaw	
gipsy/gypsy		gnome	
giraffe		gnu (animal, see knew, new)	
girate	gyrate		
girder		goad	
girdle		gobbledygook	
girth		goblet	
giser	geyser	goblin	
gist		goerd	gourd
gitar	guitar	Goethe	

gofer	gopher	granade	grenade
goggles		granary	
goiter		grandeur	
golf (game, see		grandiloquence	
gulf)		grandiose	
golosh	galosh	granite	
gondola		granular	
gonorrhea		granulate	
gopher		graphic	
gorgeous		graphite	
gormet	gourmet	grapple	
gorilla (ape, see		grate (fireplace,	
guerrilla)		see great)	
goshe	gauche	gratify	
gossamer		gratitude	
gossip		gratuity	
gouge		gratuitous	
goulash		gravity	
goulish	ghoulish	grayhound	greyhound
gourd		great (large, see	
gourmet		grate)	
gout		greed	
governable		greet	
government		gregarious	
governor		greive	grieve
gown		greivence	grievance
gracious		gremlin	
gradation		grenade	
gradient		grenadier	
gradual		grenadine	
graduate		greyhound	
grafite	graphite	gridiron	
gragarious	gregarious	grievance	
grain		grieve	
grainary	granary	grievous	
grammar		grill	

grimace
grime
grip (clutch)
grippe (infection)
grisly (horrible,
    see grizzly)
gristle
grizzly (bear, see
    grisly)
groan (moan, see
    grown)
groggy
grommet
grosgrain ribbon
grotesque
grotto
grouchy
grouse
grovel
grown (mature,
    see groan)
grudge
gruel
gruesome
grumble
guarantee (agree-
    ment)
guaranty (war-
    rant)
guard
guardian
gubernatorial
guerrilla (soldier,
    see gorilla)

guffaw
guidance
guide
guild (associa-
    tion, see gild)
guile
guillotine
guilt
guinea pig
guise (false man-
    ners, see guys)
guitar
gulf (chasm, see
    golf)
gullible
gully
gulosh   goulash
gumbo
gurgle
gutteral
guys (pl. men or
    ropes, see
    guise)
guzzle
gymnasium
gymnast
gynecology
gyp
gypsum
gypsy/gipsy
gyrate
gyration
gyroscope

H

habatat   habitat

habeas corpus

haberdashery

habitat

habitual

habitué

hacienda

hackneyed

haddock

Hagalian   Hegelian

haggard

haggle

hail (ice lumps,
   see hale)

hair (fur, see
   hare)

hairbrain   harebrain

hairy-kary   hara-kiri

halatosis   halitosis

halcyon

hale (sound,
   see hail)

halibut

halitosis

hallelujah

halliard/halyard

Halloween

hallowed

hallucination

hallucinogen

halseon   halcyon

halve

halyard/halliard

hamburger

hammer

hammock (sus-
   pended bed, see
   hummock)

hamper

handicap

handicraft

handkerchief

handle

handsome (suit-
   able, see
   hansom)

handy

hangar (plane
   port)

hanger (wire
  device)
hanker
hankerchief   handkerchief
hansom (cab, see
  handsome)
Hanukkah/
  Chanukah
hanous   heinous
haphazard
happy
hara-kiri
harangue
harass
harbinger
harbor
hardy
hare (rabbit, see
  hair)
harebrain
harem
hari-kiri   hara-kiri
harken/hearken
harlot
harmonica
harmonious
harmony
harness
harpoon
harpsichord
harrowing
harry
hart (stag, see
  heart)
harth   hearth
hartily   heartily

hary-kary   hara-kiri
harvester
hasenpfeffer
hashish
hassock
hatchet
hatred
haughty
haul
haunch
haunt
haven
haversack
havoc
hawthorn
hazardous
haze
hazelnut
heal (cure, see
  heel)
healthful
hear (heed, see
  here)
hearken/harken
hearse
heart (organ, see
  hart)
hearth
heartily
heat
heath
heathen
heather
heave
heaven
heavy

hebephrenia		hemorrhage	
heckle		hemorrhoid	
hectic		hemrige	hemorrhage
hectograph		hemroid	hemorrhoid
hedge		henceforth	
hedgemony	hegemony	henna	
hedonism		hepatitis	
heed		herald	
heel (base, see		heraldic	
heal)		herange	harangue
heeth	heath	heratage	heritage
hefty		herb	
Hegelian		herbaceous	
heffer	heifer	herbivorous	
hege	hedge	herculean	
hegemony		here (now, see	
heifer		hear)	
height		heredity	
heinous		Hereford	
heir (inheritor,		herem	harem
see air, err)		heresy	
heist		heretic	
heleum	helium	Herford	Hereford
helical		heringbone	herringbone
helicopter		herisy	heresy
heliotrope		heritage	
heliport		heritic	heretic
helium		hermaphrodite	
helm		hermetic	
helmet		hermit	
helter-skelter		hernia	
hematology		heroin (drug)	
hemisphere		heroine (female,	
hemlock		hero)	
hemoglobin		herold	herald
hemophilia		heron	

herredity	heredity	hindrance	
herringbone		hinge	
herse	hearse	hiphalutin	highfalutin
hesitate		hipnosis	hypnosis
heterodox		Hippocratic	
heterogeneous		oath	
heteronym		hippodrome	
heterosexual		hippopotamus	
heuristic		hire (employ,	
heven	heaven	see higher)	
hew (cut, see		hiroglyphic	hieroglyphic
hue)		hist	heist
hexagon		histamine	
hexameter		histology	
hiacinth	hyacinth	histrionic	
hiatus		hitherto	
hibachi		hives	
hibernate		hoar (frost, see	
hibiscus		whore)	
hibochi	hibachi	hoard (save, see	
hibred	hybrid	horde)	
hiccough/		hoarse (rough,	
hiccup		see horse)	
hideous		hoax	
hidrolic	hydraulic	hobble	
hidrangea	hydrangea	hobgoblin	
hierarchy		hockey	
hieroglyphic		hocus-pocus	
higher (taller, see		hodgepodge	
hire)		hoe	
highfalutin		hoi polloi	
hijack		hoist	
hilarious		hole (cavity, see	
him (pronoun,		whole)	
see hymn)			hooligan
himan	hymen	holiness	

hollandaise
hollow
holocaust
holster
holyness   holiness
homage
homacide   homicide
homaletic   homiletic
homany grits   hominy grits
homely
homeopath
homicide
homiletic
homily
hominy grits
homogeneous
homogenize
homologous
homonym
homosexual
Honakah   Hanukkah/
                    Chanukah
honesty
honky
honor
honorarium
hooch
hoodlum
hooligan
hootenanny
hoping (wishing)
hopping
  (jumping)
horascope   horoscope
horde (crowd,
  see hoard)

horendous   horrendous
horible   horrible
horid   horrid
horizontal
hormone
hornet
horoscope
horrendous
horrible
horrid
horror
hors d'oeuvre
horse (animal,
  see hoarse)
horticulture
hosiery
hospital
hostage
hostel (housing)
hostile (un-
  friendly)
hovel
hover
howitzer
howl
hoy paloi   hoi polloi
hubbub
huch   hooch
huckleberry
huckster
hue (color, see
  hew)
huge
hullabaloo
humador   humidor
humanitarian

humble		hydrangea
humerus (arm-		hydrant
bone, see		hydrate
humorous)		hydraulic
humid		hydrocarbon
humidor		hydrochloric
humiliate		hydrodynamics
humility		hydroelectric
humis	humus	hydrogen
hummock/		hydrogenate
hammock		hydrolic hydraulic
humor		hydrolysis
humoresque		hydrometer
humorous		hydrophobia
(funny, see		hydrotherapy
humerus)		hydroxide
humus		hyfen hyphen
hundred		hygiene
hundredth		hymen
hunger		hymn (song,
hunta	junta	see him)
hurbaceous	herbaceous	hyperbola (math)
hurbivorous	herbivorous	hyperbole
hurdle (barrier,		(overstate)
see hurtle)		hyphen
hurdy-gurdy		hypnosis
hurl		hypnotize
hurmophrodite	hermaphrodite	hypochondria
hurricane		hypocrisy
hurried		hypocrite
hurtle (collide,		hypodermic
see hurdle)		hypotension
husky		hypotenuse
hustings		hypothalamus
hustle		hypothesis
hyacinth		hypothesize
hybrid		hypothetical

hyssop

hysteria

hysterectomy

I

iambic
ibidem (ibid.)
ibis
ichthyology
icicle
icing
icon/ikon
iconoclast
iconography
ictheology   ichthyology
icumenical   ecumenical
icycle   icicle
ideal
idel   idle
identical
identify
ideology
iderdown   eiderdown
idiocy
idiom
idiomatic
idiosyncrasy
idiot
idle (useless)
idol (statue)

idolater
idolatry
idolize
idyl/idyll (poem)
igloo
igneous
ignite
ignition
ignoble
ignominious
ignoramous
ignorance
ignore
iguana
ikon/ icon
I'll (I will; see
    aisle, isle)
illegal
illegible
illegitimate
illiberal
illicit (unlawful,
    see elicit)
illimitable
illiteracy

illogical
illuminate
illusion (false
  idea, see
  allusion)
illusory
illustrate
illustrator
illustrious
ilucidate   elucidate
image
imagery
imagine
imbalance
imbalm   embalm
imbecile
imbed   embed
imbibe
imbitter   embitter
imboss   emboss
imbroglio
imbue
imitate
immaculate
immanent (in-
  dwelling, see
  eminent; immi-
  nent)
immaterial
immature
immeasurable
immediate
immemorial
immense
immerse

immersion (in
  water, see
  emersion)
inmesh/enmesh
immigrate (move
  into, see
  emigrate)
imminent (im-
  pending, see
  eminent,
  immanent)
immobile
immoderate
immodest
immolate
immoral
immortal
immune
immutable
impacted
impairment
impale
impalpable
impartial
impasse
impassioned
impassive
impatient
impeach
impeccable
impecunious
impede
impediment
impel
impend

impenetrable
impenitence
imperative
imperceptible
imperceptive
imperfect
imperial
imperious
imperishable
impermanent
impermeable
impersonal
impersonate
impertinence
imperturbable
impervious
impetigo
impetuous
impetus
impiety
impinge
impious
impish
implacable
implacement   emplacement
implant
implausible
implement
implicate
implicit
implore
imply
impolite
impolitic
imponderable

import
importable
importance
importunate
importune
impose
imposition
impossible
impostor
imposture
impotent
impound
impoverish
impractical
imprasario   impresario
imprecate
imprecise
impregnable
impregnate
impresario
impress
imprimatur
imprint
imprison
improbable
impromptu
improper
impropriety
improvident
improvise
imprudent
impugn
impulse
impunity
impute

imune   immune

in absentia

inaccessible

inaccuracy

inadequate

inadmissible

inadvertent

inadvisable

inalienable

inalterable

inamorata

inane

inanimate

inappeasable

inapplicable

inappreciable

inapproachable

inards   innards

inarticulate

inartistic

inate   innate

inattentive

inaudible

inaugural

inaugurate

inauspicious

inbed   embed

incalculable

incamptment   encampment

incandescent

incantation

incapable

incapacitate

incarcerate

incarnate

incautious

incendiary

incense

incentive

incephalitis   encephalitis

inception

incessant

incestuous

inchoate

inchant   enchant

incident

incidious   insidious

incindiary   incendiary

incinerate

incipid   insipid

incipience (early
   stage, see in-
   sipience)

incipient

incircle   encircle

incise

incision

incisive

incisor

incite (instigate,
   see insight)

inclement

inclose/enclose

incognito

incoherent

incombustible

incommensurate

incommodious

incommunicable

incommunicado

incomparable	incumber	encumber
incompass	encompass	incur
incompatible	incurable	
incompetence	indebted	
incompliant	indecency	
incomprehensible	indecipherable	
inconceivable	indecision	
inconclusive	indecisive	
incongruous	indecorum	
inconsequential	indefatigable	
inconsistent	indefeasible	
inconsolable	indefenite	indefinite
inconsonant	indefensible	
inconspicuous	indefinable	
inconstant	indefinite	
incontestable	indegent	indigent
incontinent	indego	indigo
incontrovertible	indelible	
inconvenient	indelicate	
incorporate	indemnify	
incorrect	indemnity	
incorrigible	indentation	
incorruptible	indenture	
increase	independence	
incredible	indescernible	indiscernible
incredulous	indescreet	indiscreet
increment	indescretion	indiscretion
incriminate	indescribable	
incrustation	indespensable	indispensable
incubate	indestructible	
incubator	indeterminate	
incubus	indicate	
inculcate	indict (accuse,	
inculpate	see indite)	
incumbent	indifference	

indigenous
indigent
indigestion
indignant
indigo
indiscernible
indiscreet
indiscretion
indiscribable   indescribable
indiscriminate
indispensable
indisposed
indisputable
indissoluble
indistinct
indistinguishable
indistructible   indestructible
indite (enjoin,
     see indict)
individual
indivisible
indoctrinate
indolent
indomitable
indubitable
induce
induct
indue/endue
indulge
indulgent
industrialist
industrious
inebriate
inedible
ineffable

ineffaceable
ineffective
ineffectual
inefficacious
inefficient
inelastic
inelegance
ineligible
ineluctable
inept
ineptitude
inequality
inequitable
inequity (injus-
     tice, see
     iniquity)
ineradicable
inerasable
inert
inertia
inervate   innervate
inescapable
inessential
inestimable
inevitable
inexcusable
inexhaustible
inexorable
inexpedient
inexpensive
inexperience
inexplicable
inexpressible
inextricable
infadel   infidel

infadelity	infidelity	infraction	
infallible		infrared	
infamous		infrequent	
infant		infringe	
infantesimal	infinitesimal	infuriate	
infanticide		infuse	
infantile		infusion	
infantry		ingenious	
infared	infrared	(clever, see	
infatuate		ingenuous)	
infection		ingenue/ingénue	
inferior		ingenuity	
infernal		ingenuous (inno-	
inferno		cent, see	
infidel		ingenious)	
infidelity		ingest	
infiltrate		Inglish	English
infinite		inglorious	
infinitesimal		ingot	
infinitive		ingraciate	ingratiate
infinity		ingrained	
infirmary		ingrate	
infirmity		ingratiate	
inflammable		ingredient	
inflammation		ingress	
inflate		ingross	engross
inflation		inhabit	
inflection		inhabitable	
inflexible		inhabitant	
inflict		inhalation	
influence		inhale	
influenza		inhance	enhance
influx		inharmonious	
informal		inherent	
informer		inherit	

inhesion		innimical	inimical
inhibit		innimitable	inimitable
inhibitor		inning	
inhospitable		innocent	
inhumane		innoculate	inoculate
inhume		innocuous	
iniciate	initiate	innovate	
iniciative	initiative	innovator	
inimical		innuendo	
inimitable		innumerable	
ining	inning	inoculate	
iniquity		inoffensive	
(wickedness,		inofficious	
see inequity)		inoperable	
initial		inoperative	
initiate		inopportune	
initiative		inordinate	
inject		inorganic	
injest	ingest	inovate	innovate
injoin	enjoin	inquisition	
injudicious		inquisitive	
injunction		inquisitor	
injure		insaciable	insatiable
injurious		insalar	insular
injustice		insalate	insulate
inkling		insalater	insulator
in memorium		insalin	insulin
inmesh	enmesh	insane	
inequity	iniquity	insanity	
innards		insatiable	
innate		inscrutable	
innebriate	inebriate	inseceptible	insusceptible
innertia	inertia	insecticide	
innervate		insecure	
(nerves, see		inselin	insulin
enervate)		insemination	

insensate
insense   incense
insensible
insensitive
inseparable
insephalitis   encephalitis
insert
insidious
insight (percep-
    tion, see
    incite)
insignia
insignificant
insincere
insinuate
insipid
insipience (lack
    of wisdom, see
    incipience)
insirgent   insurgent
insirmountable   insurmount-
                           able
insirrection   insurrection
insistence
insite   incite
insize   incize
insolation
insole
insolent
insoluble
insolvable
insolvency
insomnia
insomniac
insouciance
inspect

inspector
inspirational
inspirit
instability
install
installation
instant
instantaneous
instead
instigate
instigator
instinct
institute
instruct
instrument
insubordinate
insubstantial
insuceiance   insouciance
insufferable
insufficient
insular
insulate
insulin
insuperable
insupportable
insurance
insurgent
insurmountable
insurrection
insusceptible
intact
intager   integer
intangible
integer
integral
integrate

integrity	intern/interne
intellect	internecine
intelligent	interogate interrogate
intelligentsia	interpolate
intelligible	interpose
intemperate	interpret
intend	interregnum
intense	interrogate
inter	interrupt
intercede	intersect
intercept	intersperse
intercession	interstate
intercom	(between states,
intercourse	see intrastate)
interdependence	interstellar
interdict	interstice
interest	interum interim
interfere	interval
interference	intervene
interim	intervenous intravenous
interior	interweave
interlace	intestate
interlinear	intestine
interlining	intimate
interlocutor	intimidate
interloper	intolerable
intermarriage	intolerant
intermediary	intonation
intermediate	intoxicant
intermezzo	intoxicate
interminable	intractable
intermission	intramural
intermittent	(sports, see in-
intermural (be-	termural)
tween walls, see	intransigent
intramural)	intransitive

intrastate (within
   a state, see
   interstate)
intravenous
intrepid
intricacy
intricate
intrigue
intrinsic
introit
introjection
introspective
introversion
introvert
intuition
intuitive
inundate
invagle   inveigle
invalid
invaluable
invariable
invasion
invay   inveigh
invective
inveigh
inveigle
inuendo   innuendo
inventory
inveriable   invariable
inverse
inversion
invertebrate
investigator
investiture
investor
inveterate

invidious
invigorating
invincible
inviolable
inviolate
invisible
invision   envision
invitation
invocation
invoice
invoke
involuntary
involution
involve
invulnerable
inward
ioda   iota
iodide
iodine
ion
ionosphere
iota
irascible
irate
ire (anger, see
   eyre)
iridescent
iris
irksome
irony
irradescent   iridescent
irradiate
irrascible   irascible
irrational
irreclaimable
irreconcilable

irrecoverable
irredeemable
irreducible
irrefutable
irregular
irrelevant
irreligious
irremediable
irreparable
irreplacable
irrepressible
irreproachable
irresistible
irresolute
irrespective
irresponsible
irretrievable
irreverence
irreversible
irrevocable
irrigate
irritable
irritant
irritate

irruption
isinglass
island
isle (small island,
    see aisle, I'll)
islet (small is-
    land, see eyelet)
ismus   isthmus
isobar
isolate
isosceles
isotope
issue
issuing
isthmus
italic
itemize
itinerant
itinerary
its (possessive)
it's (it is)
ivory
ivy

J

jackal

jacket

jagged

jaguar

Jahovah — Jehovah

jajune — jejune

jalopy

Jambalaya

jamboree

janitor

jargon

jasmine

jaundice

jaunty

javelin

jazmine — jasmine

jealousy

jean (pants,
   see gene)

jeep

jejune

jelatin — gelatin

jelopy — jalopy

jelousy — jealousy

jeopardy

jepardy — jeopardy

jerkin (jacket,
   see gherkin)

jerrymander — gerrymander

jersey

jest (mock,
   see gest)

jesture — gesture

jettison

jetty

jewel

jewlery — jewelry

jibe/gibe

jigger

jiggle

jingo

jinks

jinrikisha

jitney

jockey

jocose

jocular

jocund

jodhpurs
joggle
joie de vivre
jollity
jondarm   gendarme
jonquil
jonre   genre
jostle
journal
journey
joust
jovial
jowl
juah de veeve   joie de vivre
jubilant
jubilation
jubilee
judge
judicate
judicial
judiciary
judicious
juditsu   jujitsu
juggernaut

juggler
jugular vein
jujitsu
julep
julienne
Jumbolaya   Jambalaya
junction
juncture
jungle
junior
juniper
junket
junta
juridical
jurisdiction
jurisprudence
jurney   journey
jurnal   journal
juror
justice
justification
juvenile
juxtapose
juxtaposition

K

kabal	cabal	kelp	
kaiak	kayak	kemona	kimono
kaiser		kenetic	kinetic
kaki	khaki	kennel	
kale		kerchief	
kaleidoscope		kernel (seed,	
kamikaze		see colonel)	
kangaroo		keropody	chiropody
kanto	canto	kerosene	
kaos	chaos	ketchup/catsup	
kapok		key (lock, see	
kapon	capon	quay)	
kaput		khaki	
karakul		kibitzer	
karat (gold, see		kidnap	
carat, caret,		kidney	
carrot)		kiln	
karisma	charisma	kilocycle	
kason	caisson	kilometer	
katsup	ketchup	kilowatt	
katydid		kimono	
kayak		kindergarten	
keask	kiosk	kindle	
keenness		kindred	

kinescope		knob	
kinesthetic		knockwurst	
kinetic		knoll	
kiosk		knot (tied rope,	
kiote	coyote	see not)	
kirsch		knowledge	
kiser	kaiser	knowledgeable	
kismet		knuckle	
kitchenette		koala	
kitty-corner/		Kodiak bear	
cater-corner		kohlrabi	
kleptomaniac		komikaze	kamikaze
knack		Koran	
knapsack		kosher	
knave (rogue,		kowtow	
see nave)		kripton	krypton
knead (mix, see		Kremlin	
need)		krone (coin, see	
knee		crone)	
kneel		kroquet	croquet
knell		krypton	
knew (to know,		kudos	
see gnu, new)		kulottes	culottes
knickers		kumin	cumin
knickknack/		kumquat	
nicknack			
knight (soldier,			
see night)			

L

labatory	laboratory	laden	
laberinth	labyrinth	lading	
labidinal	libidinal	ladle	
laborer		lager beer	
laboratory		laggard	
laborious		lagistics	logistics
labotomy	lobotomy	lagitimate	legitimate
labretto	libretto	lagoon	
labyrinth		laison	liaison
lacerate		laissez faire	
lachrymal		laity	
lachrymose		lama (monk, see	
lackadaisical		llama)	
lackey		lamanar	laminar
laconic		lamanate	laminate
lacquer		lamb	
lacrimal	lachrymal	lambaste	
lacrimose	lachrymose	lame/lamé	
lacrosse		lament	
lactation		laminar	
lactic acid		laminate	
lactose		lampion	
lacuna		lampoon	
ladder (steps,		lamprey eel	
see latter)		lancet	

landau		lathe (machine)	
language		latice	lattice
languid		latitude	
languish		latrine	
languor		latter (last, see	
lanoleum	linoleum	ladder)	
lanolin		lattice	
lanset	lancet	laturgical	liturgical
lantern		laud	
lanyard		laudanum	
lapel		laudatory	
lapidary		laugh	
lapse		launch	
laquer	lacquer	launder	
larceny		laureate	
larder		laurel	
lareat	lariat	lavaliere	
larengitis	laryngitis	lavatory	
largess		lavender	
larghetto		lavish	
largo		lawd	laud
lariat		lawdanum	laudanum
larseny	larceny	lawdatory	laudatory
larva		lawn	
laryngitis		lawyer	
larynx		laxative	
lasagna		laxity	
lascerate	lacerate	layette	
lascivious		layman	
lassitude		lazafaire	laissez faire
lasso		lazanya	lasagna
lateen sail		lazaretto	
latent		leach (to remove,	
lateral		see leech)	
latex		lead (guide or	
lath (fiberboards)		metal)	

leader		legal	
league		legate	
leak (slow loss, see leek)		legation	
		legato	
lean (incline, see lien)		leger	ledger
		legend	
lear	leer	legendary	
leash		legerdemain	
least		leget	legate
leasure	leisure	leggacy	legacy
leatard	leotard	leggings	
leather		legible	
leaven		legion	
lebedinal	libidinal	legionnaire	
Leberstraum	Lieberstraum	legislate	
lecher		legislature	
lecherous		legitimate	
leconic	laconic	legitimacy	
lectern		legon	legion
lecture		legonaire	legionnaire
led (past tense of lead)		legue	league
		legume	
leder	liter	leisure	
ledge		leitmotiv	
ledger		lemma	
leech (blood sucker, see leach)		lemming	
		lemur	
leek (herb, see leak)		length	
		lenient	
leer		lenity	
leery		lentil (plant, see lintel)	
leeward			
leeway		leopard	
		leotard	
legable	legible	lepard	leopard
legacy		leper	

lepersy	leprosy	lewd	
lepidopterous		lexicography	
leprechaun		lexicon	
leprosy		liable (responsibil-	
Lesbian		ity, see libel)	
lesion		liaison	
lesiveous	lascivious	liar (falsifier, see	
lessee		lyre)	
lesson		libary	library
lessor		libation	
letcher	lecher	libedinal	libidinal
letcherous	lecherous	libel (false state-	
leter	liter	ment, see liable)	
lether	leather	liberal	
lethal		liberate	
lethargic		libertarian	
lethargy		libertine	
lettuce		libidinal	
leucite (silicate,		libido	
see Lucite)		library	
leucocyte/leuko-		librarian	
cyte		libretto	
leukemia		librium	
leukocyte/leuco-		lice	
cyte		license	
levée (embank-		licentious	
ment, see levy)		liceum	lyceum
leven	leaven	lichen (plant, see	
leviathan		liken)	
levity		licit	
levy (tax, see		licorice	
levee)		lie (untruth, see	
lew	lieu	lye)	
leward	leeward	Lieberstraum	
leway	leeway	liege	

lien (legal, see
  lean)
lienent   lenient
lieu
lieutenant
ligament
ligature
lightening (bright-
  ening)
lightning (elec-
  tricity)
likelihood
liken (compare,
  see lichen)
lilac
lile   lisle
Lilliputian
lily
limb (appendage,
  see limn)
limber
limbo
limelight
limerick
limit
limn (draw, see
  limb)
limousine
limph   lymph
limphatic   lymphatic
limpid
Limrick   Limerick
linage/lineage
linament   liniment
linch   lynch

lineal
lineament
linear
lineate
linen
Lineotype   Linotype
lingerie
linguist
liniment
linoleum
Linotype
lintel (above
  door, see lentil)
linx   lynx
lionize
lionnaise   lyonnaise
liquefaction
liquefy
liqueur
liquidate
liquor
lisence   license
lisentious   licentious
lisine   lysine
lisis   lysis
lisit   licit
lisivious   lascivious
lisle
lissome
listen
litany
litegate   litigate
liter
literacy
literal

literature		lodge	
litergy	liturgy	loganberry	
lithe		logarithm	
lithograph		loger beer	lager beer
litigate		logical	
litmotif	leitmotiv	logistics	
litmus paper		logy	
littany	litany	loincloth	
litter		loiter	
liturgical		loneliness	
liturgy		lonely	
livelihood		longerie	lingerie
liver		longevity	
liverwurst		longitude	
livery		loom	
livid		loose	
lizard		lopsided	
llama (animal, see lama)		loquacious	
		lore	
loadstar/lodestar		Lorelei	
loadstone/lode- stone		lorengitis	laryngitis
		lose (verb, see loss)	
loam			
loathe		losenger	lozenge
lobe		loss (noun, see lose)	
loblolly pine			
lobotomy		lothe	loath
lobster		lotion	
lobule		lottery	
locket		lotus	
locomotion		lounge	
locust		louse	
locution		loutish	
lodestar/loadstar		louver	
lodestone/load- stone		lovable	
		lovaliere	lavaliere

lozenge

lubricate

lucid

Lucite (plastic,
    see leucite)

lucocyte   leucocyte

lucrative

lucre

ludicrous

luftwaffe

luggage

lugubrious

lukemia   leukemia

lull

lullaby

lumbago

lumbar (vertebra)

lumber (wood)

luminary

luminescent

luminous

lummox

lunacy

lunar

lunatic

luncheon

luncheonette

lunge

lurch

lurid

lurk

luscious

lustrous

lutenant   lieutenant

Lutheran

luver   louver

luxuriant

luxuriate

luxurious

luxury

lyceum

lye (soap, see
    lie)

lymph

lymphatic

lynch

lynx

lyonnaise

lyre (harp, see
    liar)

lyric

lysergic acid di-
    ethylamide

lysine

lysis

M

ma'am

macabre

macadam

macaroni

macaroon

macaw

macerel mackerel

machete

machination

machine

machinery

machinist

mackerel

macrocosm

macron

Macurochrome Mercuro-
      chrome

madam (English)

madame (French)

Madeira wine

mademoiselle

madonna

madras

madrigal

Madusa Medusa

maelstrom

maestoso

maestro

magazine

magenta

maggot

magistrate

magna cum laude

magnafy magnify

magnanimous

magnate (wealthy
 person, see mag-
 net)

magnatude magnitude

magnesia

magnesium

magnet (lode-
 stone, see mag-
 nate)

magnificent

magnify

magnitude

magnolia

magot maggot

maharaja

mahatma		maleria	malaria
Mah-Jongg		malestrom	maelstrom
mahogany		malevolent	
maiden		malfeasance	
mail (postal,		malformation	
see male)		malice	
maillot		malicious	
maim		malign	
main (principal,		malignant	
see mane)		maline	malign
maintain		malinger	
maître d'		malingerer	
maître d'hôtel		malisious	malicious
maize (corn, see		mall (promenade,	
maze)		see maul)	
majenta	magenta	mallard	
majesty		malleable	
Majong	Mah-Jong	maller	mauler
majority		mallet	
maladjusted		mallis	malice
malady		malmsey wine	
malaise		malnutrition	
malange	melange/	malot	mallet
	mélange	malpractice	
malaria		malstrom	maelstrom
malard	mallard	malt	
malatto	mulatto	maltase (enzyme)	
malay	melee	Maltese (language)	
malcontent		maltose (chemi-	
mal de mer		cal)	
male (mascu-		mam	ma'am
line, see mail)		mame	maim
maleable	malleable	mamen	mammon
maledy	malady	mammal	
malefactor		Mammalia	
malekite	malachite	mammary	

mammilla		manicle	manacle
mammon		manicure	
mammoth		manifest	
mamsey wine	malmsey wine	manifesto	
		manifold	
mana	manna	manipulate	
manafold	manifold	manna	
managerie	menagerie	mannaise	mayonnaise
mana ray	manta ray	mannequin	
manacle		manner (mode)	
manage		manor (mansion)	
manakin	mannequin	mansion	
mañana		manta ray	
manatee		manteia	mantilla
mandamus (writ of)		mantel (shelf, see mantle)	
mandarin		mantilla	
mandate		mantle (cloak, see mantel)	
mandatory			
mandible		manual	
mandolin		manufacture	
mane (hair, see main)		manure	
		manuscript	
maneac	maniac	manuver	maneuver
manefest	manifest	manyana	mañana
manefesto	manifesto	marabou	
manetee	manatee	maraca	
maneuver		maragold	marigold
manganate		maranade	marinade
mangle		maranate	marinate
mango		maraschino cherry	
mangy		marathon	
mania		marauder	
maniac		marawana	marijuana
manic			

Mardi gras
mare
margarine
margin
marginal
maridian   meridian
marigold
marijuana
marimba
marinade
marinate
marine
marionette
marital
maritime
marjoram
markee   marquee
marl
marlin
marmalade
marmoset
marmot
maroca   maraca
maroon
marow   marrow
marquee (at a
    theater)
marquis (royalty)
marquisette
marriage
marriageable
marrow
marry
marshal (official,
    see martial)

marshmallow
marsupial
marten (animal,
    see martin)
marter   martyr
marterdom   martyrdom
martial (warlike,
    see marshall)
martin (bird, see
    marten)
martinet
martyr
martyrdom
marvel
marvelous
marzipan
masa   mesa
masacer   massacre
masacism   masochism
mascara
mascerade   masquerade
mascot
masculine
maseur   masseur
mashanation   machination
Masiah   Messiah
masochism
masochist
mason
masquerade
massacre
massage
masseur
masseuse
massive

mastadon	mastodon	mauve
masthead		maverick
masticate		mawkish
mastiff		maxim
mastodon		maximal
mastoid		maximum
masuse	masseuse	mayhem
matador		mayonnaise
maten	matin	mayor
matenee	matinee	maze (labyrinth,
mater de	maitre d´	see maize)
material (matter)		mazurka
materiel/matériel		M.C./emcee
(equipment)		mead
maternal		meadow
maternity		meager
mathematics		mean (intend or
Mathuselah	Methuselah	middle, see
maticulous	meticulous	mein)
matier	metier/métier	meander
matin		meant
matinee		measles
matriarch		measure
matriculate		meat (food, see
matrimony		meet, mete)
matrix		mecca
matron		mechanic
matter		mechanism
mattress		medaphor metaphor
Maudigra	Mardi gras	medal (award, see
mature		metal, mettle)
maudlin		medatarsal metatarsal
maul (beat, see		meddle (interfere,
mall)		see medal,
mauler		mettle)
mausoleum		medeocer mediocre

medeocrity	mediocrity	melody
medetate	meditate	melon
media		membrane
median		memento
mediate		memoir
medical		memorabilia
medicate		memorable
medicinal		memorandum
medicine		memorial
medieval		memory
mediocre		menace
mediocrity		menage
meditate		menagerie
medium		mendacious
medley		mendicant
medow	meadow	menial
meek		meningitis
meerschaum		menopause
meet (contact,		menorah
see meat, mete)		menstruate
megacycle		menstruation
megalomania		mensuration
megaphone		mental
megaton		menthol
meger	meager	mention
melancholia		mentor
melancholy		merange	meringue
melange/mélange		mercantile
melct	mulct	mercenary
melee		mercerized thread
meleu	milieu	merchandise
melevolent	malevolent	merchant
melibdenen	molybdenum	mercurochrome
mellifluent		mercury
mellow		mercy
melodrama		

mere (pool, see
  mire)
meretricious
merganser duck
merge
meridian
meringue
merited
meritorious
mermaid
merose   morose
mershum   meerschaum
mesa
mescal
mescaline
mesdames
meskeg   muskeg
meskellung   muskellunge
mesmerize
mesquite
message
messenger
mestizo
mesure   monsieur
metabolism
metabolic
metal (iron, see
  medal, mettle)
metallurgy
metamorphic
metamorphosis
metaphor
metaphysical
metatarsal
mete (measure,
  see meat, meet)

meteor
meteorite
meteorology
meter
methadone
methane
method
methodology
methyl
methylene
meticulous
metier/métier
metric
metrical
metronome
metropolis
metropolitan
mettle (courage,
  see medal,
  metal)
mews (stables,
  see muse)
mezmorize   mesmerize
mezzanine
mezzo-soprano
miasma
mica
microanalysis
microbe
microcosm
microcosmic
micrometer
microorganism
micron
microscope
midevil   medieval

midget
midriff
midst
mien (bearing,
   see mean)
miestro   maestro
miget   midget
might (power,
   see mite)
mignonette
migraine
migrate
migration
migratory
mikado
milapede   millipede
mildew
mileage
milieu
militancy
militant
militarist
military
militia
millenary
   (1,000th anni-
   versary, see
   millinery)
milktoast   milquetoast
millennium
millet
millimeter
milliner
millinery (hats,
   see millenary)
million

millipede
millwright
milquetoast
mime
mimeograph
mimic
mimosa
minaret
minature   miniature
minastrone   minestrone
miner (mine-
   worker, see
   minor)
mineral
mineralogy
minescule   minuscule
minester   minister
minesteral   ministerial
minestration ministration
minestrone
mingle
miniature
minimum
minion
minister
minks (pl. animal,
   see minx)
minnow
minor (underage,
   see miner)
minority
minow   minnow
minstrel
mintage
minuet
minus

minuscule		misjudgment	
minute (time or small)		misletoe	mistletoe
		mismanage	
minyon	minion	misnomer	
minyonette	mignonette	misogyny	
minx (pert girl, see minks)		misque	miscue
		missal (book, see missile)	
mio	maillot	misshapen	
miopia	myopia	missile (weapon, see missal)	
miopic	myopic		
miracle		mission	
miraculous		missionary	
mirage		missive	
mire (marsh, see mere)		misspell	
meeriad	myriad	misstate	
mirr	myrrh	misstep	
mirror		mistake	
mirth		mistletoe	
mirtle	myrtle	mistoso	maestoso
misalliance		mistress	
misanthrope		misure	monsieur
miscalculation		mite (insect, see might)	
miscarriage			
miscegenation		mitigate	
miscellaneous		mitt	
mischief		mitten	
mischievous		mnemonics	
misconception		moan (complain, see mown)	
misconstrue			
miscue		moat (trench, see mote)	
misdemeanor			
miser		mobile	
miserable		moccasin	
misfeasance		modal (logic, see model)	
misinterpretation			

modecum	modicum	momento	memento
model (image, see modal)		momentous	
moderate		monacle	monocle
modernization		monaker	moniker
modes operandi	modus oper-andi	monarch	
		monastery	
		monastic	
modest		monator	monitor
modeste	modiste	monetary	
modicum		monetone	monotone
modify		monger	
modish		Mongoloid	
modist	modest	mongoose	
modiste		mongrel	
modlin	maudlin	moniker	
modulate		monitor	
modulation		monochromatic	
modus operandi		monocle	
mogul		monogamy	
mohair		monogram	
moist		monograph	
molar		monogyny	
molasses		monolithic	
Molatov cock-tail	Molotov cocktail	monologue	
		monomania	
molecular		monopoly	
molecule		monostery	monastery
molest		monosyllable	
mollify		monotheism	
mollusk		monotone	
mollycoddle		monotonous	
Molotov cock-tail		monoxide	
		monsieur	
molten		monsignor	
molybdenum		monsoon	
momentary		monster	

monstrosity	
montage	
monument	
moñana	mañana
moomoo	muumuu
moorage	
moose (animal, see mousse)	
mope	
moppet	
moral (ethics)	
morale (spirit)	
morane	moraine
morass	
moratorium	
moray eel	
morays	mores
morbid	
morcel	morsel
mordant (caustic)	
mordent (music)	
mores	
morfine	morphine
morgage	mortgage
morgue	
moribund	
morning (dawn, see mourning)	
moron	
morose	
morphine	
morphology	
morray eel	moray eel

morrow	
morsel	
moseleum	mausoleum
mortal	
mortar	
mortgage	
mortician	
mortify	
mortise	
mortuary	
mosaic	
Moselle wine	
mosey	
mosque	
mosquito	
moss	
mote (speak, see moat)	
motet	
motif	
motile	
motion	
motive	
motley	
mottled	
motto	
mountain	
mourning (grieving, see morning)	
mouse (rodent)	
mousse (dessert, see moose)	
mouton coat	
mov	mauve

mower		munitions	
mown (cut down,		mural	
see moan)		murcury	mercury
moze	mosey	murky	
Mozell wine	Moselle wine	murmur	
mucilage		murr	myrrh
mucous membrane		muscatel	
mufti		muscle (body	
mugger		tissue, see	
muggy		mussel)	
mukluk		muscular dys-	
mulatto		trophy	
mulberry		muse (meditate,	
mulch		see mews)	
mulct		museum	
mullet		mushroom	
multen	molten	musician	
multifarious		musilage	mucilage
multifold		muskellunge	
Multigraph		musket	
multilateral		musketeer	
multilinear		muskrat	
Multilith		muslin	
multipartite		mussel (shellfish,	
multiple		see muscle)	
multiple sclerosis		mustache	
multiplicand		mustard (on	
multiplicity		hot dogs)	
multitude		mustered (assem-	
mumble		bled)	
mummify		mutable	
mummy		mutilate	
mumu	muumuu	mutineer	
mundane		mutiny	
municipal		mutter	
munificent		mutton	

mutual
muumuu
muzzle
myopic
myriad
myrrh
myrtle
mysterious

mystic
mystify
mystique
myth
mythical
mythological
mythology

N

nack	knack	natal	
nacreous		natatorium	
nadir		national	
nagging		native	
naive/naïve		nativity	
naivete/naïveté		nattatorium	natatorium
namby-pamby		natty	
napalm		natural	
naphtha		nature	
napom	napalm	naughty	
napsack	knapsack	nausea	
narate	narrate	nauseate	
narcissus		nauseous	
narcissistic		nautical	
narl	gnarl	nautilus	
narcosis		nauty	naughty
narcotic		naval (navy, see	
narrate		navel)	
narrator		nave (church,	
narrow		see knave)	
nasal		navel (belly-	
nascent		button, see	
nash	gnash	naval)	
nasturtium		navigate	
nat	gnat	navigator	

naw	gnaw	nemesis	
nay (no,		nemonics	mnemonics
see neigh)		neolithic	
nazel	nasal	neomycin	
nebulous		neon	
necessary		neophyte	
necessity		nepetism	nepotism
neckerchief		neoplasm	
necklace		nephew	
necktie		nephritis	
necromancy		nepotism	
necrophilia		nerture	nurture
nectar		nervana	nirvana
nectarine		nerve	
need (require,		nervous	
see knead)		nestle	
needle		netting	
ne'er-do-well		nettle	
nefarious		neuclear	nuclear
nefritis	nephritis	neuclei	nuclei
negate		neucleon	nucleon
negative		neucleus	nucleus
neglect		neumatic	pneumatic
negligee		neumonia	pneumonia
negligent		neural	
negligible		neuralgia	
negotiate		neuritis	
negotiation		neurology	
negotiator		neurosis	
Negro		neurotic	
Negroes		neuter	
neice	niece	neutral	
neigh (horse,		neutron	
see nay)		new (recent, see	
neighbor		gnu, knew)	
neither		newel	

nexus		nipple	
niacin		nippy	
nicatine	nicotine	nirvana	
nicety		nisei	
niche		nisi	
nickel		nitch	niche
nickelodeon		nitrate	
nickers	knickers	nitric acid	
nicknack/knick-		nitrify	
knack		nitrite	
nickname		nitrogen	
nicotine		nitroglycerin	
nictitropism	nyctitropism	nob	knob
niece		noble	
niether	neither	nobility	
nieve	naive/naïve	noblesse oblige	
nievete	naivete/	nockwurst	knockwurst
	naïveté	nocturnal	
nifarious	nefarious	nocturne	
niggardly		nocuous (injuri-	
night (evening,		ous, see noxious)	
see knight)		node	
nightingale		nodule	
nihilism		noel/noël	
nimbes	nimbus	noggin	
nimble		noise	
nimbus		noll	knoll
nimonics	mnemonics	nomad	
nimph	nymph	nom de plume	
nimphomaniac	nympho-	nome	gnome
	maniac	nomenclature	
nine		nominal	
nineteen		nominate	
ninety		nominclature	nomenclature
ninth		nominee	
niponese	nipponese	nonabsorbent	

nonacceptance
nonaggressive
nonalcoholic
nonbeliever
nonbelligerent
nonblooming
noncense   nonsense
nonchalance
noncoercive
noncombatant
noncombustible
noncommissioned
noncommittal
noncommunist
noncompetitive
noncompliance
nonconductor
nonconformist
noncontroversial
noncorrosive
nondescript
none (nothing,
  see nun)
nonelective
nonentity
nonessential
nonexistence
nonfiction
nonintervention
nonirritant
nonmetallic
nonobjective
nonobsorbent   nonabsorbent
nonpareil
nonpartisan
nonpoisonous

nonproductive
nonprofit
nonrenewable
nonreoccuring   nonrecurring
nonresident
nonrestrictive
nonsectarian
nonsense
non sequitur
nontaxable
nontoxic
nonvascular
nonviolence
noodle
no one
noose
normal
normalcy
nosea   nausea
noseate   nauseate
nostalgia
nostril
nostrum
not (negative,
  see knot)
notable
notarize
notary
notation
notch
noteriety   notoriety
noteworthy
notible   notable
notical   nautical
notice
noticeable

noticing		numb	
notify		number	
notilus	nautilus	numbskull	numskull
notion		numerable	
notoriety		numeral	
notorious		numerous	
no-trump		numismatics	
nougat		numskull	
nought		nun (clergy,	
nourish		see none)	
novacain	novocaine	nuptial	
novel		nural	neural
novelette		nuralgia	neuralgia
novelist		nurish	nourish
novena		nuritis	neuritis
novice		nurology	neurology
novitiate		nurosis	neurosis
novocaine		nurotic	neurotic
noxious (causing		nurvana	nirvana
harm, see		nurse	
nocuous)		nursery	
nozzle		nurture	
nth degree		nusance	nuisance
nuance		nuter	neuter
nubile		nutmeg	
nuckle	knuckle	nutral	neutral
nuclear		nutrient	
nuclei		nutrition	
nucleus		nutritious	
nudity		nutron	neutron
nugat	nougat	nuzzle	
nugget		nylon	
nuisance		nymph	
null		nymphomaniac	
nullify			

O

oafish
oaken
oar (paddle, see
  or, ore)
oasis
oath
obalisk   obelisk
obasance   obeisance
obbligato
obcequies   obsequies
obcequious obsequious
obcidian   obsidian
obdurate
obedient
obeisance
obelisk
obese
obesity
obey
obfuscate
obituary
objection
objector
objet d'art
oblate

oblation
obligate
obligato   obbligato
obligatory
oblige
oblique
obliterate
oblivion
oblivious
oblong
obloquy
obnoxious
oboe
oboist
obortion   abortion
obscene
obscond   abscond
obscurantism
obscure
obscurity
obsequies
obsequious
observant
observation
observatory

observe
obsess
obsession
obsidian
obsolescent
obsolete
obsolve   absolve
obsorb   absorb
obstacle
obstain   abstain
obstanate   obstinate
obstatrician   obstetrician
obstenancy   obstinacy
obstetrical
obstetrician
obstetrics
obstinacy
obstinate
obstreperous
obstruct
obstructer
obsurd   absurd
obtain
obtrude
obtrusive
obtuse
obverse
obviate
obvious
ocarina
occasion
occelot   ocelot
occident (the
    west, see
    accident)

occidental
occipital
occlude
occlusion
occular   ocular
occulist   oculist
occult
occultism
occupant
occupation
occupy
occur
occurred
occurrence
ocean
oceanic
oceanography
ocelot
ocher
ocident   occident
ocidental   occidental
ocipital   occipital
ociput   occiput
o'clock
oclude   occlude
oclusion   occlusion
octagon
octagonal
octahedron
octane
octave
octet
octogenarian
octopus
octoroon

ocular		ofiolatry	ophiolatry
oculist		often	
ocult	occult	oftener	
ocultism	occultism	ogle	
ocupant	occupant	ogre	
ocupation	occupation	ogreish	
ocur	occur	ohm	
ode		oiliness	
od infinitum	ad infinitum	oily	
odious		ointment	
od nauseam	ad nauseam	okay	
odometer		okra	
odor		old lange zine	auld lang syne
odoriferous		oldster	
odorous		oleaginous	
odulation	adulation	oleander	
od valorem	ad valorem	oleomargarine	
odyssey		oleoresin	
Oedipus		olfactory	
oestrus/estrus		oligarchy	
ofel	offal	Olympic	
ofen	often	om	ohm
offal		omega	
offend		omelet	
offender		omen	
offense		ominous	
offensive		omission	
offertory		omlet	omelet
officer		omnibus	
official		omnipotent	
officialdom		omnipresent	
officiate		omniscient	
officiator		omnivorous	
officious		omph	oomph
offset		onanism	

oncoming		operation	
oncore	encore	operative	
onerous		operator	
ongenue	ingenue/	operetta	
	ingénue	opertune	opportune
onion		ophthalmologist	
onís	onus	opiate	
onix	onyx	opine	
onnomatopoeia	onomato-	opinion	
	poeia	opinionated	
onnus	onus	opium	
onomatopoeia		oponent	opponent
onslaught		oportunism	opportunism
onsomble	ensemble	oportunity	opportunity
ontological		opose	oppose
ontology		oposite	opposite
ontrepreneur	entrepreneur	oposition	opposition
ontourage	entourage	oppertune	opportune
onus		oppertunity	opportunity
onward		oppesite	opposite
onyx		opponent	
oogenesis/		opportune	
oögenesis		opportunistic	
oolong		opportunity	
oomph		oppose	
ooze		opposite	
opacity		opposition	
opal		oppossum	
opalescent		oppress	
opaque		oppression	
opel	opal	opprobrious	
opelescent	opalescent	opprobrium	
opera		oppulence	opulence
operable		opress	oppress
operate		opression	oppression

opt

optamism   optimism

opthamologist   ophthalmol-
                      ogist

optic

optical

optician

optimism

optimistic

optimum

option

optional

optometrist

optometry

opulence

opus

or (conjunction,
  see oar, ore)

oracle (wise man,
  see auricle)

oracular

oral (vocal, see
  aural)

orange

orangutan

orate

orator

oratorio

oratory

orbit

orbital

orcestra   orchestra

orchard

orchestra

orchid

ordain

ordeal

or d'erve   hors d'oeuvre

ordinal

ordinance (law, see
  ordnance)

ordinarily

ordinary

ordinate

ordnance
  (weapons, see
  ordinance)

ordure

ore (metal, see
  oar, or)

oregano

oreomycin   aureomycin

oreole   oriole

orfice   orifice

organ

organdy

organic

organism

organist

organization

organize

organizer

organza

orgasm

orgiastic

orgy

oricle   oracle

orient

oriental

orientation

orifice		osicle	ossicle	
origin		osiloscope	oscilloscope	
original		osmosis		
origination		osmotic		
originator		osprey		
oriole (bird, see		ossicle		
aureole)		ossification		
orison		ossify		
orlon		ossillate	oscillate	
ornament		ossilloscope	oscilloscope	
ornamental		ossine	oscine	
ornamentation		ossprey	osprey	
ornate		ossulate	osculate	
ornathology	ornithology	ostensible		
orneriness		ostentation		
ornery		ostentatious		
ornithology		osteopath		
orphan		ostracism		
orphanage		ostracize		
orracle	oracle	ostrich		
orratorio	oratorio	ostricism	ostracism	
orregano	oregano	ostricize	ostracize	
or revoir	au revoir	ostrige	ostrich	
orrifice	orifice	otiose		
orriole	oriole	otter		
orrison	orison	ought (should,		
ortopsy	autopsy	see aught)		
orthodontist		oui (yes, see we)		
orthodoxy		Ouija board		
orthogenic		ounce		
orthopedics		ourselves		
oscillate		oust		
oscilloscope		outboard		
oscine		outburst		
osculate		outdistance		

outmoded
outpatient
outpouring
outrage
outrageous
outrigger
outsell
outward
outweigh
outwit
ova
ovary
ovation
overalls
overawed
overbearing
overboard
overconfident
overdose
overdraft
overexposure
overhaul
overlap
overruling

overseas
overseer
oversight
overt
overture
overweening
overwhelming
overwrought
overy   ovary
oviparous
ovulate
ovum
owe
owing
owlish
ownership
oxeye daisy
oxidation
oxide
oxidize
oxtail
oxygen
oyster
ozone

P

pabulum
pacemaker
pachyderm
pacific (calm)
Pacific (time or
  ocean)
pacifier
pacify
package
packet
packsack
packsaddle
packyderm   pachyderm
pact
paculiar   peculiar
pacuniary   pecuniary
padding
paddle
paddock
padestrian   pedestrian
padlock
padock   paddock
padre
padrone

paean (song, see
  paeon, peon)
paeon (syllables,
  see paeon,
  peon)
pagan
paganism
pageant
pageantry
pagination
pagoda
pail (bucket, see
  pale)
pain (hurt, see
  pane)
painstaking
paintbrush
painting
pair (two, see
  pare, pear)
pairing (grouping,
  see pareing)
Paisley print
pajama

palace		palor	pallor
paladin		palpable	
paladium	palladium	palpitate	
palamino	palomino	palsy	
palatable		paltry (see	
palatal		poultry)	
palate (mouth,		palygamy	polygamy
see palette,		palzy	palsy
pallet)		pamflet	pamphlet
palatial		pamfleteer	pamphleteer
palaver		pampas	
palbearer	pallbearer	pamper	
pale (white,		pamphlet	
see pail)		pamphleteer	
palea		panacea	
paleate	palliate	panaroma	panorama
paleolithic		panatella	
paleontology		panchromatic	
paletal	palatal	pancreas	
palette (art		panda	
board, see pal-		pandemic	
ate, pallet)		pandemonium	
palfrey		pander	
palid	pallid	pandowdy	
palisade		pane (glass, see	
palitable	palatable	pain)	
palladium		panegyric	
pallbearer		panel	
pallet (bed, see		paneply	panoply
palate, palette)		panhandle	
palliate		panic	
pallid		panicky	
pallor		pannacea	panacea
palmistry		pannel	panel
palomino		panoply	

panorama		paradox	
pansy		parafenalia	parapher-
pantaloon			nalia
pantemine	pantomime	paraffin	
pantheism		parafrase	paraphrase
pantheon		paragon	
panther		paragoric	paregoric
panties		paragraph	
panting		parakeet	
pantomime		parallax	
pantry		parallel	
panty		parallelogram	
pantywaist		paralysis	
Panzer division		paralytic	
panwah	peignoir	paralyze	
papacy		paramecium	
papal		parameter	
papaw		paramount	
papaya		paramour	
papecy	papacy	paramutuel	parimutuel
papier-mache/		paranoia	
papier-maché		parapalegic	paraplegic
papilla		parapet	
papirus	papyrus	paraphernalia	
papoose		paraphrase	
paprika		paraphrastic	
papyrus		paraplegic	
parable		parapsychology	
parabola		parashute	parachute
parachute		parasite	
paracite	parasite	parasol	
paraclete		parasympathetic	
parade		paratrooper	
paradigm		parboil	
paradise		parcel	

parcheesi		parler	parlor
parchment		parley (confer-	
pardon		ence, see	
pardonable		parlay)	
pare (peal, see		parliament	
pair, pear)		parliamentarian	
parecide	parricide	parliamentary	
paregoric		parlor	
parent		Parmesan cheese	
parentage		parmigeon	ptarmigan
parenthesis		parochial	
parenthetic		parody (imita-	
paresis		tion, see parity)	
par excellence		parol (oral)	
parfay	parfait	parole (release)	
parfait		paroxysm	
pariah		parquet	
paridy	parity	parricide	
	(equality)/	parrot	
	parody	parry	
	(imitation)	parsel	parcel
parietal		parshal	partial
parimutuel		parsimony	
paring (cutting,		parsing	
see pairing)		parsley	
parish		parsnip	
parishioner		parson	
paristalsis	peristalsis	parsonage	
paritonitis	peritonitis	parterre	
parity (equality,		partesan	partisan
see parody)		parthenogenesis	
parka		partial	
parlance		participate	
parlay (bet, see			
parley)			

participial
participle
particle
particular
partisan
partisipate   participate
partition
partner
partridge
parusal   perusal
parvenu
pary   parry
paschal
pasha
pasify   pacify
Pasley print   Paisley print
paso   peso
pasqueflower
passable
passage
passe/passé
passerby/passer-by
passion
passionate
passive
passtime   pastime
pastachio   pistachio
paste
pastel
pasteurize
pastiche
pastime
pasting

pastor
pastorate
pastoral (rural
  life)
pastorale (music)
pastrami
pastry
pasturage
pasture
pasturize   pasteurize
pasty
patchwork
pate de foie gras/
  pâté de foie
  gras
patella
paten (plate, see
  patten)
patent (protec-
  tion)
paterfamilias
patern   pattern
paternal
paternity
paternoster
pathetic
pathology
pathos
patience (toler-
  ance)
patients (clients)
patina
patio

patisserie	
patois	
patren	patron
patreot	patriot
patriarch	
patriarchal	
patrician	
patrimony	
patriot	
patrol	
patron	
patronage	
patronize	
patronymic	
patroon	
patten (shoe, see	
paten)	
patter	
pattern	
patty shell	
patuitary	pituitary
patunia	petunia
paucity	
paunchy	
pauper	
pause	
pavement	
pavilion	
paving	
pawnbroker	
payola	
peace (calm, see	
piece)	
peach	
peacock	
pea jacket	

peak (top, see	
peek, pique)	
peal (ring, see	
peel)	
peanut	
pear (fruit, see	
pare, pair)	
pearl (gem, see	
purl)	
peasant	
pebble	
pecable	peccable
pecant	peccant
pecan	
peccable	
peccadillo	
peccant	
peccary	
pecon	pecan
pectin	
pectoral	
peculiar	
pecuniary	
pedacure	pedicure
pedagree	pedigree
pedagogue	
pedagogy	
pedal (lever, see	
peddle)	
pedament	pediment
pedantic	
peddle (sell, see	
pedal)	
pedegogue	pedagogue
pedegogy	pedagogy
pedentic	pedantic

pedestal		penance	
pedestrian		penant	pennant
pediatrician		penate	pennate
pediatrics		pence	
pediatrist	podiatrist	penchant	
pedicure		pencil	
pedigree		pendant (orna-	
pediment		ment)	
pedistal	pedestal	pendent (hanging	
pedology		down)	
pee jacket	pea jacket	pendulum	
peek (peep, see		penecillin	penicillin
peak, pique)		penetent	penitent
peel (strip, see		penetential	penitential
peal)		penetrate	
peenockle	pinochle	penetrable	
peer (an equal,		penguin	
see pier)		penicillin	
peerless		peninsula	
peeve		penitent	
peewee		penitential	
peignoir		penitrate	penetrate
pejorative		penmanship	
Pekingese		pennance	penance
pekoe		pennant	
pelagic		pennate	
pelaver	palaver	pennicillia	penicillin
pelican		penniless	
pellet		penninsula	peninsula
pell-mell		penochle	pinochle
pelvic		penology	
pelvis		penorious	penurious
pemento	pimento	pension	
pemmican		pentagon	
penal		pentahedron	
penalty		pentameter	

pentateuch		perceptible	
pentathlon		perch	
Pentecostal		perchance	
pentegon	pentagon	perchase	purchase
penthouse		percieve	perceive
penuche		percipient	
penuchle/		percipitate	precipitate
pinochle		percolate	
penultimate		percussion	
penurious		perdicament	predicament
penury		perdition	
penwah	peignoir	perdurable	
peon (worker, see		peregrinate	
paean, paeon)		peremptory	
peonage		pereneum	perineum
peony		perennial	
pepilla	papilla	perentheses	parentheses
pepper		perenthesis	parenthesis
pepsin		perenthetic	parenthetic
peptone		perfect	
pequant	piquant	perfectible	
peracycle	pericycle	perfecto	
peralysis	paralysis	perfer	prefer
peralytic	paralytic	perfidy	
perambulate		perforate	
peramecium	paramecium	perforce	
perameter	parameter	perform	
peranha	piranha	perfume	
per annum		perfunctory	
perapatetic	peripatetic	pergure	perjure
percale		perhaps	
per capita		periah	pariah
perceive		pericycle	
percent		periferal	peripheral
percentage		perifery	periphery
percept		perigee	

perihelion		perpetual	
peril		perpetuate	
perilous		perpetuity	
perimeter		perpindicular	perpendicular
perineum		perplex	
period		perport	purport
periodical		perscription	prescription
peripatetic		persecute	
peripheral		persecutor	
periphery		perservative	preservative
periscope		perserve	preserve
perish		perseverance	
perishable		persevere	
peristalsis		persiflage	
peritonitis		persimmon	
periwinkle		persipient	percipient
perjure		persist	
perjury		persistence	
perky		personable	
permanent		personage	
permeable		personal (per-	
permeate		son, see person-	
permissible		nel)	
permission		persona non grata	
permissive		personify	
permit		personnel (em-	
permutation		ployes, see per-	
pernicious		sonal)	
perochial	parochial	perspective	
perogative	prerogative	perspectus	prospectus
perorate		perspicacious	
perouette	pirouette	perspicacity	
peroxide		perspicuity	
perpatuity	perpetuity	perspire	
perpendicular		persuade	
perpetrate		persuant	pursuant

persuasion		pettiness	
persue	pursue	petty	
	pursuit	petuitary	pituitary
pertain		petulance	
pertinacious		petulant	
pertinent		petunia	
perturb		Peugeot	
perturbable		pewter	
pertussis		pfennig	
peruke		phalanx	
perusal		phallic	
pervade		phallus	
perverbial	proverbial	phantom	
perverse		pharmaceutical	
pervert		pharmacology	
perywinkle	periwinkle	pharmacy	
pesel	pestle	pharynx	
peso		phase (facet, see	
pessimism		faze)	
pesticide		pheasant	
pestiferous		phenobarbital	
pestilent		phenomenon	
pestle		phenomenal	
petal		phenotype	
petard		philanderer	
petcock		philanthropy	
petella	patella	philately	
petite		philharmonic	
petition		Philipino	Filipino
petit jury		philippic	
petits fours		philodendron	
petits pois		philology	
petrify		philosophy	
petroleum		philter (potion,	
petrology		see filter)	
petticoat		phlegm	

phlegmatic	physician
phlogistic	physics
phobia	physiognomy
phobic	physiology
phoebe	physiotherapy
phonetic	physique
phonics	pianist
phonograph	piano
phosphate	piasano
phosphorescence	piazza
phosphorus	pibold piebald
photo	pica
photoelectric	picaresque
photoengraving	picayune
photogenic	piccalilli
photograph	piccolo
photography	pickerel
photogravure	picket
photomural	pickle
photon	pickyune picayune
photosensitive	picnic
photosphere	picnicking
photostat	pictograph
photosynthesis	pictorial
phototaxis	picture
phototropic	picturesque
phrase	picuniary pecuniary
phraseology	piddling
phrenetic/frenetic	pidgin English
phrenology	(language, see
phylogeny	pigeon)
phylum	piebald
physic	piece (segment,
physical (about	see peace)
bodies, see	piece de resistance/
fiscal)	pièce de résis-
	tance

piedmont

pier (dock, see
  peer)

pierce

piety

pigeon (bird, see
  pidgin)

pigment

pigmy   pygmy

pigsty

pilage   pillage

pilaster

pilchard

pilfer

pilgrim

pilgrimage

piling

pillage

pillar

pillory

pillow

pilon   pylon

pilorus   pylorus

pilot

pimento

pimpernel

pimple

pinacle   pinnacle

pinafore

pinate   pinnate

pince-nez

pincers

pineal gland

pineapple

pininsula   peninsula

pinnace

pinnacle

pinnate

pinochle/penuchle

pinsers   pincers

pinultimate   penultimate

pioneer

piorrhea   pyorrhea

pious

pipe

pipette

piping

piquant

pique (provoke
  or score, see
    peak, peek)

piranha

piracy

pirate

pirex   pyrex

pirosis   pyrosis

pirouette

piscatorial

pistachio

pistil (flower
  part)

pistol (gun)

piston

pitapat

pitch

pitcher

piteable   pitiable

piteous

pithy

pitiable

pitiful

pitiless

piton

pittance

pittapat   pitapat

pituitary

pity

pivot

pixy

pizza

pizzeria

plabian   plebian

placable

placard

placate

placebo

placement

placenta

placible   placable

placid

plack (coin, see
  plaque)

placket

plagerist   plagiarist

plagiarism

plagiarist

plagiary

plague

plaid

plain (flat, see
  plane)

plaint

plaintiff (suer)

plaintive (mourn-
  ful)

plait (briad, see
  plate)

plaiting (to braid,
  see plating)

plane (geometry,
  see plain)

planet

planetary

planograph

plantain

plantation

plaque (plate,
  see plack)

plasebo   placebo

plasid   placid

plasma

plaster

plastic

plasticity

platapus   platypus

plate (dish, see
  plait)

plateau

platen

plater   platter

platetude   platitude

platform

plating (to coat,
  see plaiting)

platinum

platitude

platoon

platten   platen

platter

platypus

plaudit		plumber	
plausible		plume	
plaza		plumer	plumber
plazma	plasma	plummet	
plea		plunder	
plead		plunge	
pleasant		pluperfect	
please		plural	
pleasure		plurality	
pleat		plurisy	pleurisy
plebian		plutocracy	
plebiscite		plutonium	
plecenta	placenta	plyers	pliers
pledge		pneumatic	
plenary		pneumonia	
plenipotentiary		poacher	
plenteous		pocket	
plesant	pleasant	podiatrist	
plete	pleat	podium	
pleurisy		poem (verse,	
plexus		see pome)	
pliable		poet	
pliant		poetic	
pliers		poet laureate	
plight		pogrom	
plinth		poh	
plistocene	pleistocene	poi	
plodit	plaudit	poignancy	
plotter		poignant	
plowshare		poinsettia	
plucky		pointillism	
plum (fruit, see		poison	
plumb)		poker	
plumage		polar	
plumb (weight,		polarization	
see plum)		Polaroid	

pole (stick, see poll)		polonaise	
		poltice	poultice
polemic		poltroon	
poler	polar	poltry	poultry
polerization	polarization	polyandry	
Poleroid	Polaroid	polychromatic	
polestar		polyclinic/poli-clinic	
polety	polity		
pole vault		polyethylene	
polex	pollex	polygamy	
policeman		polyglot	
policlinic/poly-clinic		polygon	
		polygyny	
policy		polyhedron	
poliglot	polyglot	polyp	
polinate	pollinate	polyphonic	
polio		polytechnic	
poliomyelitis		pomade	
polip	polyp	pome (fruit, see poem)	
polish			
polite		pomegranate	
political		pommel (saddle, see pummel)	
politico			
politics		pompadour	
polity		pompano	
polka		pompon	
poll (voting place, see pole)		pompous	
		pomposity	
pollen		poncho	
pollex		ponder	
pollinate		pongee	
polliwog		pon-ne	pince-nez
pollute		pontiff	
pollution		pontifical	
Pollyanna		pontoon	
pollywog	polliwog	pony	

poo	pooh	porselain	porcelain
poodle		portable (move-	
poor (needy, see		able, see potable)	
pore, pour)		portage (carry	
poper	pauper	overland, see	
popery		pottage)	
poplar (tree, see		portal	
popular)		porteco	portico
poplin		portege	portage
popourri	potpourri	portend	
poppy		portent	
populace (masses,		portfolio	
see populous)		portico	
popular (approved,		portion	
see poplar)		portly	
populate		portrait	
Populist		portray	
populous (thickly		porus	porous
settled, see		posess	possess
populace)		poshion	potion
porcelain		posit	
porcupine		position	
pore (small		positive	
opening, see		posse	
poor, pour)		possess	
poriferous		possible	
porige	porridge	possum	oppossum
pornographic		postage	
pornography		postal	
porous		poster	
porosity		posterior	
porpoise		posterity	
porpus	porpoise	posthaste	
porridge		posthumous	
Porsche		postimpressionism	

postmortem
postnatal
postorbital
postponable
postponement
postscript
postulate
postumous   posthumous
posture
posy (flower,
   see posse)
potable (drink-
   able, see port-
   able)
potage   pottage
potash
potassium
potation
potato
potency
potent
potentate
potential
potery   pottery
potion
potlatch
potpourri
pottage (soup,
   see portage)
pottery
poultice
poultry
pounce
pound
pour (flow,
   see pore, poor)

pousse-café
poverty
powder
power
powwow
pox
pozit   posit
pozy   posy
practicable
practical
practice
practitioner
pragmatic
prairie
praise (admire,
   see prase)
praline
prance
prankish
prarie   prairie
prase (stone, see
   praise)
prasentable   presentable
prasume   presume
prate
prattle
prawn
pray (plead, see
   prey)
prayer
preach
preacher
preamble
precancel
precarious
precaution

precede

precedent (first,
 see president)

precept

precinct

precind   prescind

precious

precipice

precipitant

precipitate

precis/précis
 (summary)

precise (exact)

precision

preclude

preclusion

precocious

preconception

precondition

precursor

predator

predecessor

predelection predilection

predestination

predetermine

predetor   predator

predicament

predicate

predict

predictable

predilection

predispose

predominant

pre-eminent/-
 preeminent

pre-empt

preen

pre-existence

prefabricate

preface

prefect

prefer

preferable

preferred

preform   perform

pregnancy

pregnant

prehensile

prehistoric

preiminent pre-eminent/-
      preeminent

prejudice

prelate

preliminary

prelude

premature

premedical

premeditate

premenition premonition

premier (official,
 see premiere,
 primer)

premiere (first
 showing, see
 premier, primer)

premise

premium

premolar

premonition

premonitory

prenatal

preoccupy

preordain
prepare
preponderance
preportion   proportion
prepose   propose
preposition
prepossessing
preposterous
prerequisite
prerogative
presage
Presbyterian
presbytery
prescience
prescind
prescribe
prescription
presdadigitation   prestidigita-
                    tion
present
presentable
presentiment
presentment
preservation
preservative
preserve
preside
president (chief,
  see precedent)
presidio
presidium
presinct   precinct
presind   prescind
presious   precious
presipice   precipice
pressure

prestidigitation
prestige
presto
presume
presumption
presumptuous
presuppose
presure   pressure
pretend
pretender
pretense
pretentious
preternatural
pretext
prettify
pretty
pretzel
prevail
prevalent
prevaricate
prevent
preverbial   proverbial
preview
previous
previso   proviso
prevoke   provoke
prey (victom, see
  pray)
pricipitant   precipitant
pricipitate   precipitate
prickle
prideful
priest
prig
priggish
primacy

prima donna		prize	
prima facie		probable	
primal		probate	
primarily		probation	
primary		probe	
primate		probiscis	proboscis
primer (first text,		probity	
see premier,		problem	
premiere)		proboscis	
primeval		procedural	
primitive		procedure	
primogeniture		proceed	
primordial		procenium	proscenium
primrose		process	
principal (main		procession	
teacher; see		proclaim	
principle)		proclivity	
principally		proconsul	
principle (general		procrastinate	
truth, see prin-		procreate	
cipal)		proctor	
principled		procure	
printable		prodegy	prodigy
prior		prodigal	
prioress		prodigious	
priority		prodigy	
prisidium	presidium	produce	
prism		product	
prison		profalactic	prophylactic
pristine			(device)
prittify	prettify	profilaxis	prophylaxis (the
privacy			prevention
private			of disease)
privilege		profane	
privy council		profanity	

profecy	prophecy (noun), prophesy (verb)	prohibit	
		prohibition	
		project	
		projectile	
profer	proffer	projector	
profess		prolactin	
profession		proletariat	
professor		proliferate	
profetic	prophetic	prolific	
proffer		prolix	
proficiency		prologue	
proficient		promenade	
profilactic	prophylactic (device)	promentory	promontory
		prominence	
profilaxis	prophylaxis (the prevention of disease)	promiscuity	
		promiscuous	
		promise	
		promissory	
profile		promolgate	promulgate
profit (gain, see prophet)		promontory	
		promote	
profitable		prompt	
profligate		promulgate	
profound		promulgator	
profundity		pron	prawn
profuse		prone	
profusion		pronoun	
progenitor		pronounce	
progeny		pronunciation	
prognosis		propaganda	
program		propagate	
programing/pro- gramming		propagation	
		propane	
progress		propeganda	propaganda
progressive		propel	

propellant
propeller
propensity
proper
property
prophalactic   prophylactic
                       (device)

prophalaxis   prophylaxis
                       (the preven-
                       tion of
                       disease)
prophecy (noun,
   see prophesy)
phophesier
prophesy (verb,
   see prophecy)
prophet (pre-
   dictor, see profit)
prophetic
prophylactic (de-
   vice)
prophylaxis (the
   prevention of
   disease)
propinquity
propitiate
propitious
proponent
proportion
propose
proposition
propound
proprietor
propriety
propulsion

prorate
prosaic
prosaically
proscenium
proscribe
prosecute
proselyte
prosenium   proscenium
prosody
prospect
prospectus
prosper
prosperity
prosperous
prostate (gland,
   see prostrate)
prostitute
prostrate (prone,
   see prostate)
prosy
protagonist
protazoan   protozoan
protean (change-
   able, see pro-
   tein)
protecol   protocol
protect
protectorate
protege/protégé
protein (chemical,
   see protean)
pro tempore
protest
Protestant
protocol

proton
protoplasm
prototype
protozoan
protrude
protrusion
protuberance
provecation   provocation
provender
proverb
proverbial
provide
providence
providential
province
provincial
provision
proviso
provocation
provocative
provoke
provost marshal
prowess
prowler
proximity
proxy
prozaic   prosaic
prozy   prosy
prude
prudent
prurient
prussic acid
psalm
psalmody
pseudo

pseudonym
psoriasis
psychedelic
psychiatry
psychic
psychoanalysis
psychoanalyze
psychodelic   psychedelic
psychodrama
psychological
psychology
psychometry
psychopathic
psychosis (illness,
    see sycosis)
psychosomatic
psychosurgery
psychotherapeutics
psychotherapy
ptarmigan
pterodactyl
ptomaine
puberty
pubic
public
publication
publicist
publicity
publicize
publish
pucker
pudding
puddle
pudgy
pueblo

puerile
puerility
puffy
Pugeot   Peugeot
pugilist
pugnacious
puissance
pulchritude
pulchritudinous
pullet
pulley
pulmonary
pulpit
pulque
pulsate
pulverize
puma
pumice
pummel (beat,
   see pommel)
pumpernickel
pumpkin
punative   punitive
punctilious
punctual
punctuate
puncture
pundit
pungent
punish
punitive
punster
pupa
pupil
puppet

puppy
purchase
purfidy   perfidy
puree/purée
purgatory
purge
purifier
Puritan
puritanical
purl (to knit,
   see pearl)
purlieu
purloin
purple
purport
purpose
purr
purse
purser
purslane
pursuant
pursue
pursuit
purvey
purview
pusillanimous
puter   pewter
pustule
put (place, see
   putt)
putrefy
putrescent
putrid
putt (golf stroke,
   see put)

puttee (leg cloth)
putty (for fixing
  windows)
puzzle
pygmy
pylon
pylorus
pyorrhea
pyramid

pyre
Pyrex
pyrites
pyromaniac
pyrosis
pyrotechnics
Pyrrhic victory
python

Q

quackery

quadragenarian

quadrangle

quadrant

quadrilateral

quadroon

quadruped

quadruple

quaff

quagmire

quail

quaint

qualify

qualitative

quality

qualm

quandary

quantify

quantity

quantum

quarantine

quarrel

quarry (excava-
tion, see query)

quarter

quartet

quarto

quartz

quasar

quasijudicial/
quasi-judicial

quatrain

quaver

quay (wharf, see
key)

quazar   quasar

quean (wench,
see queen)

queasy

queen (woman
ruler, see quean)

queer

quell

quench

querulous

query (question,
see quarry)

quest

question

questionnaire

quetzal	quirk
queue (line, see cue)	quisine cuisine
quibble	quisling
quiddity	quit (end, see quiet, quite)
quid pro quo	quite (total, see quiet, quit)
quien sabe	
quiescent	quiver
quiet (silent, see quit, quite)	quixotic
	quizling quisling
quietus	quizzed
quince	quizzical
quinine	quoin (building angle, see coign, coin)
quintessence	
quintet	
quintuple	quonset
quipped	quorum
quipster	quota
quire (25 sheets, see choir)	quotient

R

rabbet (groove,
  see rabbit,
  rarebit)
rabbi
rabbinical
rabbit (animal,
  see rabbet,
  rarebit)
rabble
rabid
rabies
raccoon
racconteur   raconteur
rachet   ratchet
racial
racist
racket
racketeer
racoon   raccoon
raconteur
racy
rader   raider
radeum   radium
radeus   radius
radei   radii

radial
radiant
radiate
radiator
radical
radii
radioactive
radiology
radiosensitive
radiosonde
radiotherapy
radish
radium
radius
raffia
raffish
raffle
ragamuffin
ragatta   regatta
ragged
raglan
ragweed
raider
raillery
railroad

raiment	
rain (water, see reign, rein)	
raindeer	reindeer
raise (elevate, see raze)	
raisin	
raith	wraith
raja	
rakish	
ralere	raillery
rally	
rambler	
ramekin	
rament	raiment
ramification	
rampage	
rampant	
rampart	
ramshackle	
rancid	
rancor	
rancorous	
random	
rankle	
ransack	
ransid	rancid
ransom	
rant (rave, see rent)	
rapacious	
rapid	
rapier	
rapine	
rapped (hit, see rapt, wrapped)	

rapport	
rapscallion	
rapsody	rhapsody
rapt (intent, see rapped, wrapped)	
rapture	
rapturous	
raquiem	requiem
rarebit (cheese dish, see rabbet, rabbit)	
rarefy	
rarely	
rarity	
rasberry	raspberry
rascal	
rasher	
rasin	raisin
raspberry	
rasping	
ratchet	
rathskeller	
ratify	
ratifier	
ratio	
ratiocination	
rational (reasonable)	
rationale (basis)	
rationalize	
ratskeller	rathskeller
rattan	
rattle	
raucous	
ravage	

ravel		reaper	
ravenous		reappearance	
ravine		reappoint	
ravioli		rearmament	
ravish		rearrange	
raw		reason	
rayon		reassemble	
raze (demolish,		reassign	
see raise)		reassure	
razor		reath	wreath
razzle-dazzle		reawaken	
reabsorb		rebate	
reactionary		rebellion	
reactor		rebirth	
read (under-		rebuff	
stand, see reed)		rebuke	
readable		rebus	
readily		rebut	
readjustment		rebuttal	
readmission		recalcitrant	
readmit		recallable	
readmittance		recant	
ready		recap	
reaf	reef	recappable	
reaffirm		recapitulate	
reagent (sub-		recede	
stance, see		receipt	
regent)		receive	
real (true, see		recency	
reel)		recent	
realistic		recepe	recipe
reallocation		receptacle	
realm		reception	
realtor		receptor	
realty		recesitate	resuscitate
ream		recession	

recidivism		recoup
recind	rescind	recourse
recipe		recovery
recipient		recreant
reciprocate		recreation
reciprocity		recrimination
recision		recrudescence
recission	rescission	recruit
recitation		rectal
recite		rectangle
reck	wreck	rectify
reckon		rectilinear
reclaim		rectitude
reclamation		rector
recliner		rectory
recluse		rectum
recognize		recumbent
recoil		recupe · recoup
recollect		recuperate
recommend		recur
recommit		recurrence
recompense		recycle
reconasance	reconnais-	redeem
	sance	redemption
reconcile		redevelopment
recondite		rediculous · ridiculous
reconnaissance		redily · readily
reconnoiter		redingote
reconsider		rediscovery
reconsign		redolent
reconsile	reconcile	redouble
reconstitute		redound
reconstruction		redress
reconvene		reduce
reconvert		redundant
record		reduplication

reed (stem, see read)	refuge
reef	refugee
reek (smell, see wreak)	refund
reel (spin, see real)	refurbish
reelect	refuse
reem ream	refusal
reemergence	refute
reemploy	regal (splendid)
reenact	regale (feed)
reengage	regalia
reenlistment	regard
reenter	regatta
reestablish	regemen regimen
reexamine	regement regiment
referable	regeneration
referee	regent (ruler, see reagent)
reference	regergitate regurgitate
referendum	regicide
referral	regime
referred	regimen
refine	regiment
refinery	region
reflect	register
reflector	registrant
reflex	registrar
reforestation	registry
reformation	regius
reformatory	regress
refract	regret
refractory	regrettable
refrain	regular
refrigerate	regulate
	regurgitate
	rehabilitate

rehearse		relieve	
reign (rule, see		religion	
rain, rein)		relinquish	
reimbursement		relish	
rein (straps, see		relm	realm
rain, reign)		relocation	
reincarnation		reluctant	
reindeer		remady	remedy
reinforcement		remain	
reinsert		remainder	
reinstate		remand	
reintegrate		remarkable	
reintroduce		remarriage	
reinvest		remedial	
reissue		remedy	
reiterate		remember	
reject		remembrance	
rejoice		remenisce	reminisce
rejoinder		reminder	
rejuvenate		reminisce	
rekindle		remiss	
relapse		remit	
relate		remittable	
relative		remittance	
relavant	relevant	remittor	
relax		remnant	
relay		remonstrate	
release		remorse	
relegate		remote	
relent		removable	
relevant		removal	
reliable		remuneration	
reliant		ren	wren
relic		renagade	renegade
relief		renaissance	

rench	wrench	repercussion	
render		repertoire	
rendezvous		repertory	
rendition		repetition	
renegade		rephrase	
renege		replaca	replica
renegotiate		replace	
renewal		replenish	
renig	renege	replete	
rennet		repletion	
renominate		replica	
renovate		reply	
renown		report	
rent (each		reportorial	
month, see		repose	
rant)		repository	
rentgen	roentgen	repossess	
renunciation		reppercussion	repercussion
reoccupy		reprehend	
reorganization		repremand	reprimand
reostat	rheostat	represent	
repair		repress	
reparation		repression	
repartee		repressive	
repast		reprieve	
repatoire	repertoire	reprimand	
repatory	repertory	reprisal	
repayable		reproach	
repeal		reprobate	
repeat		reproduce	
repel		reproduction	
repellent		reproof	
repent		reptile	
repentance		republic	
reper	reaper	repudiate	
reperation	reparation	repugnant	

repulse
repulsive
reputable
reputation
request
requiem
requirement
requisite
requital
requite
resale
resavoir   reservoir
rescind
rescission
rescue
research
resedue   residue
resemble
resent
reseprocity   reciprocity
resergent   resurgent
reserrect   resurrect
reservation
reserve
reservoir
resesitate   resuscitate
reside
residence (home,
  see residents)
resident
residential
residents
  (dwellers, see
  residence)
residual
residivism   recidivism

residue
resign
resilient
resin
resist
resister (one who
  resists)
resistor (elec-
  trical)
resolution
resolve
resonance
resort
resound
resource
respect
respectable
respective
respiration
respiratory
respite
resplendent
response
responsible
responsive
rest (sleep, see
  wrest)
restaurant
restaurateur
restitution
restive
restoration
restrain
restrant   restaurant
restrict
result

resultant

resume

resumption

resurgent

resurrect

resuscitate

retail

retaliate

retard

retch (vomit,
  see wretch)

retention

reticent

retina

retire

retna   retina

retoric   rhetoric

retort

retract

retread

retrial

retribution

retrieve

retroactive

retrocession

retrogression

retrospect

retroversion

revalle   reveille

reveal

revear   revere

reveille

revel

revelation

revelry

revenge

revenue

reverberate

revere

reverent

reverie

reverse

reversion

revert

review (go over,
  see revue)

revile

revise

revision

revitalize

revival

revivify

revocable

revoke

revolution

revolver

revue (skits, see
  review)

revulsion

reward

rezilient   resilient

rhapsody

rheostat

rhetoric

rheumatic

rheumatism

rheumatoid

rhinestone

rhinitis

rhinoceros

rhombus
rhubarb
rhyme (poetry,
    see rime)
rhythm
ribald
ribbing
ribbon
riboflavin
riccochet   ricochet
rickets
rickey
rickrack
ricksha
ricochet
riddance
riddle
ridge
ridicule
ridiculous
riffle (ripple, see
    rifle)
riffraff
rifle (gun/ran-
    sack, see riffle)
rift
rigamarole/rig-
    marole
riga mortis   rigor mortis
rige   ridge
right (true, see
    write, rite,
    wright)
righteous
rigid

rigidity
rigmarole/riga-
    marole
rigor
rigor mortis
rigorous
rime (frost, see
    rhyme)
rinestone   rhinestone
rinitis   rhinitis
rinoceros   rhinoceros
rinse
riot
ripcord
ripen
ripple
rise
riskay   risque
risky
risotto
risque/risqué
rite (ritual, see
    right, wright,
    write)
ritualistic
rival
rivalry
rivulet
roach
roam (wander,
    see Rome)
roan
roar
roast
robbery

robin		root	
rocketry		Roquefort cheese	
rococo		Rorschach test	
rocous	raucous	rosary	
rodent		roseate	
rodeo		Rosetta stone	
roe (doe, see		rosette	
row)		Rosh Hashana	
roentgen		Roshock test	Rorschach test
rogue		rosin	
roil		roster (roll, see	
roister		rooster)	
Rokfort cheese	Roquefort cheese	rostrum	
		rotary	
role (function)		rotate	
roll (roster)		rotenone	
rollicking		rotery	rotary
roly-poly/rolypoly		rotisserie	
romaine lettuce		rotogravure	
romance		rotosection	
rombus	rhombus	rotten	
Rome (city, see		rotund	
roam)		rotunda	
romper		roue/roué	
rompus room	rumpus room	roudy	rowdy
rondeau (poem,		rouge	
see rondo)		rough	
rondevous	rendezvous	roulette	
rondo (music, see		roundelay	
rondeau)		rouse	
rookery		rout (expel)	
rookie		route (road)	
roommate		routine	
rooster		row (paddle, see	
(chicken, see		roe)	
roster)		rowdy	

royal		rumage	rummage
rozeate	roseate	rumatic	rheumatic
Rozetta stone	Rosetta stone	rumatism	rheumatism
rozin	rosin	rumatoid	rheumatoid
rua	roue/roué	rumba	
Rubaiyat		rumble	
rubarb	rhubarb	ruminant	
rubber		rummage	
rubbish		rummy	
rubble		rumor	
rubella		rumple	
Rubiat	Rubaiyat	rumpus room	
rubric		runcible spoon	
ruche		rupee	
rucksack		rupture	
ruction		rural	
rudder		ruse	
ruddy		russet	
rude		Russell (name,	
rudiment		see rustle)	
rue		rustic	
ruen	ruin	rustle (sound or	
ruff	rough	steal, see	
ruffian		Russell)	
ruffle		rutabaga	
rugged		rutine	routine
ruin		rythm	rhythm
ruinous		rye (seed, see	
ruler		wry)	
rulette	roulette		

S

sabatage	sabotage	sacroiliac	
Sabbath		sacrosanct	
sabbatical		sacum	succumb
saber		saddle	
sable		sadist	
sabotage		sadistic	
saboteur		safari	
sac (pouch in animal, see sack)		safety	
		saffron	
		safire	sapphire
saccharine		saga	
sacede	secede	sagacious	
sacession	secession	sagebrush	
sachel	satchel	sahib	
sachet		sail (canvas, see sale)	
sack (bag, see sac)		salacious	
sackcloth		salad	
sacral		salamander	
sacrament		salami	
sacred		salary	
sacrifice		salatary	salutary
sacrilegious		sale (selling, see sail)	
sacristy			

salecism	solecism	sanatorium	
salenium	selenium	(health resort,	
salient		see sanitarium)	
saline		sanctify	
salinity		sanctimonious	
saliva		sanction	
salivate		sanctuary	
sallow		sandal	
salm	psalm	sandwich	
salmagundi		sane (rational,	
salmon		see seine)	
salon (room)		sang-froid	
saloon (bar)		sanguine	
salstice	solstice	sanitarium	
salubility	solubility	(hospital, see	
salubrious		sanatorium)	
salutary (reme-		sanitary	
dial, see soli-		sanity	
tary)		sanpan	sampan
salutation		Sanskrit	
salute		sans serif	
salvage (save,		sanwich	sandwich
see selvage)		saonce	seance
salvation		sapena	subpoena
salve		sapient	
salvo		sapodilla	
samantics	semantics	sapphire	
sameri	samurai	sapsago	
samon	salmon	sarape/serape	
samovar		sarcasm	
sampan		sarcastic	
sample		sarcophagus	
samurai		sardine	
sanata	sonata	sardonic	
sanatary	sanitary	sargasso	

sargent	sergeant	sav	salve
sari		savage	
sarong		savanna	
sarsaparilla		savant	
sartorial		savior	
sashay	sachet	savoir-faire	
sasheate	satiate	savor	
sasparilla	sarsaparilla	savoy	
sassafras		sawyer	
satallite	satellite	saxophone	
satanic		scabbard	
satchel		scabrous	
sate		scaffold	
sateen		scalawag	
satellite		scald (what boil-	
sater	satyr	ing water does,	
saterist	satirist	see scold)	
saternine	saturnine	scale	
satiate		scalene	
satin		scallion	
satire		scallop	
satirist		scalp	
satisfaction		scalpel	
satisfy		scaly	
satual	satchel	scamper	
saturate		scan	
saturnine		scandalize	
satyr		scanty	
sauce		scapegoat	
sauerkraut		scapula	
sauna		scar	
saunter		scarce	
sausage		scarcity	
saute/sauté		scare	
sauterne		scarf	

scarlet
scathe
scatterbrain
scavenge
scenario
scene
scenery
scent (odor, see
  cent, sent)
scents (pl. odors,
  see cense, cents,
  sense)
scepter
scerge   scourge
scerrilous   scurrilous
scervy   scurvy
schedule
schematic
scheme
scherzo
schism
schizoid
schizophrenia
schmaltz
schnapps
schnauzer
scholar
scholastic
schooner
schottische
schuss
sciatic nerve
science
scimitar
scintillate

scion
scissor
sclerosis
scoff
scold (reprimand,
  see scald)
scooter
scope
scorch
scorn
scorpion
scoundrel
scour
scourge
scowl
scrabble
scramble
scratch
scrawl
scrawny
scream
screech
screen
scribble
scribe
scrimmage
scrimp
script
scripture
scroll
scrotum
scrounge
scruff
scruple
scrupulous

scrutinize

scuba

scuff

scuffle

sculduggery   skulduggery

scull (boat, see
    skull)

scullery

scullion

sculptor

sculptural

scuppernong

scurrilous

scurry

scurvy

scuttle

scuttlebutt

scythe

sea (ocean,
    see see)

seam (sewing, see
    seem)

seaman (sailor,
    see semen)

seamstress

seance

sear (burn, see
    seer)

search

searra   sierra

searsucker   seersucker

season

secede

secession

seclude

secondary

secrecy

secret (mystery,
    see secrete)

secretary

secrete (give off,
    see secret)

secretive

sect

sectarian

section

sector

secular

secure

security

sedament   sediment

sedan

sedate

sedative

sedentary

sedge

sediment

sedition

seduce

sedulous

see (perceive,
    see sea)

seed (grain, see
    cede)

seem (appear, see
    seam)

seemly

seepage

seer (prophet, see
    sear)

seersucker

seesaw

seethe

sege   sedge

segment

segregate

seine (net, see
  sane)

seismograph

seize

seizure

selacious   salacious

seldom

select

selenium

self-confidence

self-conscious

self-discipline

self-evident

self-explanatory

self-expression

self-indulgence

self-preservation

self-reliance

self-respect

self-righteous

self-sacrifice

selfsame

self-satisfied

seller (person,
  see cellar)

selvage (edge,
  see salvage)

semantics

semaphore

semblance

semelina   semolina

semen (sperm,
  see seaman)

semester

semiautomatic

semicircle

semicolon

semifinalist

seminal

seminar

seminary

semiphore   semaphore

semiprecious

Semitic

semmetry   symmetry

semolina

sena   senna

senario   scenario

senate

senator

senile

senior

senna

senor/señor

sensation

sense (intelli-
  gence, see
  cense, cents,
  scents)

senses (sensations,
  see census)

sensitive

sensitize

sensory

sensual
sensuous
sent (dispatched,
  see cent, cense,
  scents)
sentament   sentiment
sentence
sentenal   sentinel
sententious
sentience
sentiment
sentinel
sentry (guard,
  see century)
separate
sepia
septer   scepter
septet
septic
septuagenarian
septum
sepulcher
sepulchral
sequel
sequence
sequential
sequester
sequin
sequoia
seraglio
serape/sarape
seraphim
serch   search
sercumb   succumb
serefim   seraphim

serenade
serendipity
serene
serenity
serf (slave, see
  surf)
serfdom
serge (fabric,
  see surge)
sergeant
serial (sequence,
  see cereal)
series
serif
serious
sermon
serpent
serpentine
serrated
serrogate   surrogate
serulean   cerulean
serum
servant
service
servicability
servile
sesame seed
sesarean   cesarean
sesquicentennial
sesquipedalian
session (meeting,
  see cession)
set-to
settee
settle

suer (one who   shamois   chamois
  sues, see   shampoo
  sewer)   shamrock
sevenfold   shamus
seventeen   shananigans   shenanigans
seventy   shanghai
sever (cut, see   Shangri-La
  severe)   shantecleer   chanticleer
several   shantung
severance   shanty (cabin,
severe (serious,   see chantey)
  see sever)   sharecropper
sewage   shartreuse   chartreuse
sewer (drain, see   shatish   schottische
  suer)   shatter
sew (mend, see   shawl
  so, sow)   sheaf
sextet   shear (cut, see
sexton   sheer)
sexual   sheath
sfagnum   sphagnum   sheek   sheik (Arab
sfelte   svelte   leader) chic
shabby   (stylish)
shackle   sheef   sheaf
shaddock   sheen
shadow   sheer (pure, see
shady   shear)
shalac   shellac   sheik (Arab
shalacked   shellacked   leader, see chic)
shale   shellac
shalee   challis   shellacked
shallot   shenanigans
shallow   shenel   chenille
shaman   shenyon   chignon
shambles   shepherd

sher	shirr	shrapnel	
sherbet		shred	
sheriff		shrew	
sherivere	charivari	shrewd	
sherry		shriek	
sheth	sheath	shrimp	
shevron	chevron	shrine	
shibboleth		shrink	
shicanery	chicanery	shrivel	
shifon	chiffon	shroud	
shifonier	chiffonier	shrub	
shield		shrubbery	
shillelagh		shuck	
shimmer		shudder	
shimmy		shuffle	
shingle		shun	
shirk		shuss	schuss
shirr		shutter	
shister	shyster	shuttlecock	
shivalry	chivalry	shyster	
shivere	charivari	sianamide	cyanamide
shiver		sianide	cyanide
shoal		siatic nerve	sciatic nerve
shoddy		sibilant	
shone (lighted,		sibling	
see shown)		sicamore	sycamore
shoot (discharge,		sicophant	sycophant
see chute)		sidereal	
shol	shoal	siege	
shorn		sierra	
shoulder		siesta	
shovel		sieve	
shower		sifless	syphilis
shown (displayed,		sifon	siphon
see shone)		sigh	

sight (see cite, site)		simultaneous	
sign		sinagogue	synagogue
signafy	signify	sincerely	
signal		sincerity	
signature		sinch	cinch
signet (seal, see cygnet)		sincopate	syncopate
		sindicate	syndicate
significant		sinecure	
signify		sinergism	synergism
silacate	silicate	sinester	sinister
silacon	silicon	sinew	
silage		singe	
silence		singleton	
silf	sylph	singular	
silhouette		sinister	
silicate		sink (submerge, see sync)	
silicon		sinnabar	cinnabar
sillogism	syllogism	sinner	
silo		sinod	synod
siloette	silhouette	sinopsis	synopsis
silvan	sylvan	sintax	syntax
simbiosis	symbiosis	sintillate	scintillate
simbiotic	symbiotic	sinuous	
simetar	scimitar	sinue	sinew
simian		sinus	
similar		sion	scion
simile		Sioux (Indians, see sou, sue)	
similitude		siphon	
simmer		sircum	succumb
simplicity		siren	
simplification		siringa	syringa
simposium	symposium	siringe	syringe
simulate		sirloin	
simulcast			

sisal		skittles	
sisegy	syzygy	skitzoid	schizoid
sissor	scissor	skitzophrenia	schizophrenia
sistern	cistern	sklerosis	sclerosis
sitadel	citadel	skulduggery	
sitar		skulk	
site (place, see cite, sight)		skull (head, see scull)	
sith	scythe	skullery	scullery
sitter		skullion	scullion
situate		skunk	
situation		slalom	
sitz bath		slander	
sive	sieve	slattern	
sivet	civet	slauch	slouch
sixpence		slaughter	
sixteenth		slavery	
sixth		slay (kill, see sleigh)	
sixty			
sizemograph	seismograph	sleazy	
sizzle		sledge	
skane	skein	sleek	
skeet		sleet	
skein		sleeve	
skeleton		sleezy	sleazy
skepernong	scuppernong	sleigh (sled, see slay)	
skerge	scourge		
skertzo	scherzo	sleight of hand (tricky, see slight)	
sketch			
skewer			
skimpy		slenderize	
skipper		sleuth	
skirmish		slew	
skism	schism	slight (frail, see sleight)	
skittish			

slight of hand   sleight of
                           hand
slippage
slippery
sloe (plum,
   see slow)
sloe-eyed
sloe gin
slogan
slolum   slalum
sloop
slope
sloppy
sloth
slouch
slough
slovenly
slow (not
   quick, see sloe)
slow-eyed   sloe-eyed
slow gin   sloe gin
sluce   sluice
sludge
slue   slew
sluggard
sluggish
sluice
slurp
slur
sluth   sleuth
smattering
smear
smelt
smirch
smirk

smite
smithereens
smock
smolder
smooth
smorgasbord
smother
smudge
smuggle
snafu
snail
snapper
sneakers
sneer
sneeze
sniffle
snippet
snitch
snivel
snooze
snorkel
snuggle
so (as a result,
   see sew, sow)
soar (fly high, see
   sore)
soared (flew, see
   sword)
sobriety
sobriquet
soccer
society
sociology
socket
sodality

sodden		solstice	
sodemy	sodomy	solubility	
soder	solder	soluble	
sodium		solution	
sodium hydroxide		solvent	
sodium nitrate		somatic	
sodium pento- thal		sombrero	
sodomy		some (portion, see sum)	
sofism	sophism	somersault	
soggy		somnambulist	
soilage		somniferous	
soiree		son (male child, see sun)	
sojourn			
solace		sona	sauna
solar		sonata	
solarium		sonic	
solar plexus		sonnet	
solataire	solitaire	sonorous	
solatary	solitary	sonter	saunter
solder		soothe	
soldier		soothsayer	
sole (shoe, see soul)		sooty	
solecism		sophism	
soledarity	solidarity	sophisticate	
solemn		sophistry	
solemnity		sophomore	
solicit		soporific	
solicitude		soprano	
solidarity		soral	sorrel
solidify		sorcery	
soliloquy		sord	sword
solitaire		sordid	
solitary (alone, see salutary)		sore (tender, see soar)	
		sorghum	

soriasis	psoriasis	spasmodic	
sorority		spastic	
sorrel		spatial	
sorsery	sorcery	spatter	
sortie		spatula	
sot		spawn	
sou (French		speach	speech
coin, see Sioux,		speal	spiel
sue)		spearmint	
soubrette		specamen	specimen
souffle/soufflé		specie	
sought		specific	
soul (spirit, see		specify	
sole)		specimen	
soup		specious	
soupcon/soupçon		speckled	
source		spectacle	
sourkraut	sauerkraut	spectacular	
souse		spectator	
souvenir		specter	
sovereign		spectral	
sow (plant, see		spectroscope	
sew, so)		spectrum	
soybean		speculate	
spacial	spatial	speech	
spacious		speed	
spacific	specific	speedometer	
spaghetti		spelunk	
spangle		spermaceti	
spaniel		spermatocyte	
spanner		spesamen	specimen
sparkle		spew	
sparrow		sphagnum	
sparse		sphere	
spasm		sphincter	
spatchla	spatula	sphinx	

spicket   spigot   sprain
spicy   sprawl
spiel   spread
spigot   spright
spikelet   sprocket
spinach   spruce
spinal   spurious
spindle   sputnik
spinet   sputter
spinneret   squab
spinster   squabble
spiral   squadron
spiritual   squalid
   (religion)   squall
spirituel (re-   squalor
   fined)   squander
spiteful   squash
spittle   squat
spittoon   squaw
spleen   squawk
splendid   squeak
splendor   squeal
splice   squeamish
splinter   squeegee
sponge   squeeze
sponsor   squirm
spontaneity   squirrel
spontaneous   squirt
spoor (trail,   stability
   see spore)   staccato
sporadic   stadium
spore (seed, see   stagnant
   spoor)   stagnate
spouse

staid (dignified,
  see stayed)
stair (step, see
  stare)
stake (spike,
  see steak)
stalactite
stalagmite
stalemate
stallion
stalwart
stamen
stamina
stammer
stampede
stanchion
standard
stanza
staple
stare (look,
  see stair)
starve
static
stationary (fixed)
stationery
  (paper)
statistics
statue
stature
status
statute
statutory
stayed (remained,
  see staid)

steadfast
steady
steak (beef, see
  stake)
steal (purloin, see
  steel)
stealth
steam
steel (metal, see
  steal)
steep
steeple
steer
stein
stellar
stelth   stealth
stencil
stenographer
stenotype
stentorian
step (walk)
steppe (plain)
stereophonic
stereopticon
stereoscope
stereotype
sterile
sterling
stern
sternum
stethoscope
stevedore
steward

stich (line of
   verse, see stitch)
stickler
stifle
stigma
stile (steps, see
   style)
stilted
stimie   stymie
stimulant
stimulate
stimulus
stipend
stipple
stiptic   styptic
stipulate
stirrup
stitch (sewing,
   see stich)
stockinet
stodgy
stogie
stoic
stolid
stolwort   stalwart
stomach
stooge
stoop (bend, see
   stoup, stupe)
stoup (large
   glass, see stoop,
   stupe)
stowaway
straddle

straight (direct,
   see strait)
strainer
strait (waterway,
   see straight)
strangle
strangulation
strategy
stratify
stratosphere
stratum
stratus
strawberry
streak
stream
strenuous
streptococcus
streptomycin
strewn
striate
stricken
stricknine   strychnine
stricture
strident
stringent
stroller
strontium
structure
strudel
struggle
strumpet
strychnine
stubborn
stucco

studious
stultify
stupe (medicated
  cloth, see
  stoop, stoup)
stupefy
stupendous
stupor
sturgeon
stutter
style (mode,
  see stile)
stylus
stymie
styptic
suacide   suicide
suade   suede
suave
subaltern
subret   soubrette
subconscious
subcontractor
suberb   suburb
subjugate
subjunctive
sublease
sublimate
sublime
subliminal
submarginal
submarine
submerge
submerse
submission

submit
subnormality
subordinate
suborn
subpoena
subscribe
subscription
subsedize   subsidize
subsedy   subsidy
subsequent
subservient
subsidiary
subsidize
subsidy
subsistence
subspecies
substance
substantial
substantiate
substantive
substitute
substratum
subterfuge
subterranean
subtle
subtropical
suburb
subversive
subvert
sucatash   succotash
succeed
success
succinct

suing		succor (relief, see	
suitable		sucker)	
suite (group,		succotash	
see sweet)		succulent	
succumb		suitor	
suceptible	susceptible	sulfa	
sucinct	succinct	sulfanilamide	
sucker (fish, see		sulfate	
succor)		sulfer	sulfur/sulphur
suction		sulfide	
sudden		sulfite	
sudo	pseudo	sulfur/sulphur	
sudonym	pseudonym	sullen	
sue (law, see		sulphur/sulfer	
Sioux, sou)		sultan	
suer (one who		sultry	
sues, see sewer)		sum (total, see	
suede		some)	
suet		sumac	
suffacate	suffocate	sumersault	somersault
suffer		summary (brief)	
sufferage	suffrage	summery (like	
sufferance		summer)	
suffice		summit	
sufficient		summon	
suffix		sumptuous	
suffle	souffle/	sun (star, see son)	
	soufflé	sundae (ice cream)	
suffocate		Sunday (Sabbath)	
suffrage		sunder	
suffuse		supena	subpoena
sufice	suffice	super	
suficient	sufficient	superabundance	
sugar		superannuate	
suggestible		superb	
suicide		supercilious	

superego
superficial
superfluous
superimpose
superintendent
superior
superlative
supernumerary
supersaturate
supersede
supersession
supersonic
superstition
superstructure
supervise
supine
supper
supplant
supple
supplement
suppliant
supplicate
supply
support
suppose
supposition
suppository
suppress
supremacy
supreme
supress   suppress
supson   soupcon/
                                     soupçon
surcease
surcharge
surely

surf (waves,
   see serf)
surfeit
surge (wave,
   see serge)
surgeon
surgery
surly
surmise
surmount
surname
surpass
surplice
surplus
surprise
surrealism
surrender
surreptitious
surrey
surrogate
surround
surseas   surcease
surveillance
survey
survive
susceptible
susinct   succinct
suspect
suspend
suspender
suspension
suspicion
sustaining
sustenance
sutable   suitable
sutle   subtle

suture   sycophant
suvenir   souvenir   sycosis (hair
svelte   disease, see
swabber   psychosis)
swagger   syllable
swain   syllabus
swallo (slug)   syllogism
swallow (bird)   sylph
swami   sylvan
swaree   soiree   symbiosis
swarthy   symbiotic
swashbuckler   symbol (sign, see
swastika   cymbal)
swatch   symbolism
swatter   symmetry
swave   suave   sympathy
swear   symphony
sweat   symposium
sweater   symptom
sweepstake   synagogue
sweet (sugar,   sync (abbr., syn-
  see suite)   chronize, see
swelter   sink)
swerve   synchromesh
swimmer   synchronize
swindler   syncopate
swine   syndicate
swirl   syndrome
switch   synergism
swivel   synod
swizzle   synonym
swollen   synonymous
sword (weapon, see   synopsis
  soared)   syntax
sycamore   synthesis

synthetic   syringe
syphen   siphon   syphless   syphilis
sypher (joint,   sysegy   syzygy
  see cipher)   systalic
syphilis   system
syringa   syzygy

T

tabacco tobacco
tabasco
taber tabor
tabernacle
tableau
tabloid
tabogan toboggan
taboo
tabor
tabular
tabulate
tabulation
tabulator
tacit
taciturn
tackle
tact
tactics
tactile
taffeta
tail (end, see
 tale)
tailor (clothes
 maker, see
 Taylor)

taint
talc
talcum
tale (story, see
 tail)
talisman
talkative
tallon talon
tallow
tallyho
Talmud
talo tallow
talon
tamarack
tambourine
tandamount tantamount
tandem
tangel tangle
tangent
tangential
tangerine
tangible
tangle
tankard
tannery

tantalize		taupe (color, see	
tantamount		tope)	
tantrum		taut (stretched,	
taper (narrow,		see taught)	
see tapir)		tautology	
tapestry		tavern	
tapioca		tawdry	
tapir (animal,		taxi	
see taper)		taxidermist	
tapistry	tapestry	Taylor (name, see	
tappioca	tapioca	tailor)	
tarantula		tea (drink, see	
tardy		tee)	
tare (weed, see		teakwood	
tear)		team (squad, see	
taregon	tarragon	teem)	
target		tear (rip, see tare)	
tariff		tear (cry, see tier)	
tarnish		teara	tiara
tarpaulin		tease	
tarpon		teat	
tarragon		teathe	teethe
tarriff	tariff	teatmouse	titmouse
tarry		teatotaler	teetotaler
tartar		tebercular	tubercular
tartare sauce		teberculosis	tuberculosis
tasit	tacit	technical	
tasiturn	taciturn	technician	
tassel		Technicolor	
tattered		technique	
tattle		technology	
tattoo		tedious	
taught (did		tedium	
teach, see taut)		tee (peg, see tea)	
taunt		teekwood	teakwood

teem (swarm, see
   team)
teeth (pl. tooth)
teethe (cut teeth)
teetotaler
telecast
telegraph
teleology
telepathy
telescope
telescopic
teletype
temerity
temper
tempera (painting
   medium, see
   tempura)
temperament
temperance
temperate
temperature
temperize   temporize
temperment temperament
tempest
tempestuous
tempis fugit tempus fugit
template
temple
temporal
temporarily
temporary
temporize
tempt
temptable
temptation

tempura (Japan-
   ese dish, see
   tempera)
tempus fugit
tenable
tenacious
tenacity
tenacle   tentacle
tenament   tenement
tenant
tendency
tendentious
tender
tenderloin
tendon
tendril
Tenebrae
tenement
tenible   tenable
tennable   tenable
tennacious tenacious
tennant   tenant
tennis
tenor
tense
tensile strength
tension
tensor
tantacle
tentative
tenterhooks
tenuous
tenure
tepee
tepid

tequila		testament	
terantula	tarantula	testicle	
terban	turban	testify	
terbine	turbine	testimonial	
terbulent	turbulent	testimony	
tereen	tureen	testosterone	
terific	terrific	tetanus	
termagant		tete-a-tete/tête-á-tête	
terminable		tether	
terminal		tetrachloride	
terminate		tetrahedron	
terminology		tetralogy	
terminus		tetrameter	
termite		tetrarch	
termoil	turmoil	Teutonic	
tern (bird, see		textile	
turn)		textual	
terodactyl	pterodactyl	textural	
terquoise	turquoise	texture	
terrace		thalamus	
terra cotta		thalidomide	
terrain		than (comparative,	
terramycin		see then)	
terrapin		thatched	
terrazzo		thealogian	theologian
terrestrial		thearetical	theoretical
terrible		theater/theatre	
terrier		theif	thief
terrific		their (poss. see	
terrify		there, they're)	
territorial		theism	
territory		theistic	
terror		theive	thieve
terse		thematic	
tertiary		theme	

then (at another
    time, see than)
thence
theocracy
theologian
theology
theorem
theoretical
theorist
theorize
theory
theosophy
therapeutic
therapy
there (place,
    see their,
    they're)
thermal
thermodynamics
thermometer
thermonuclear
thermos
thermostat
therum   theorem
thesaurus
thesis
thesorus   thesaurus
Thespian
they're (they are,
    see their, there)
thiamine
thicket
thief
thieve
thigh
thimus   thymus

thirsty
thirteen
thirtieth
thirty
thistle
thither
thoracic
thorax
thorobred   thoroughbred
thorough (com-
    plete, see
    through)
thoroughbred
though
thought
thousand
threadbare
threaten
thresher
threshold
thrice
throat
throes (pain,
    see throws)
thrombosis
throttle
through (pene-
    trate, see thor-
    ough)
throws (does
    throw, see
    throes)
thug
thumb
thunderous
thursty   thirsty

thwart
thyme (herb, see
  time)
thymus
thyroid
tiara
tic (twitch)
tick (sound)
ticket
tickle
ticktacktoe
ticoon   tycoon
tidal
tiddlywinks
tier (row, see
  tear)
tigress
tike   tyke
tile
timbal (drum)
timbale (food)
timber (wood)
timbre (sound)
time (minute,
  see thyme)
timidity
timorous
timpani (drum,
  see tympany)
timpany   tympany
tin
tincel   tinsel
tincture
tine
tinge
tingle

tinsel
tintinnabulation
tiny
tiphoid   typhoid
tiphoon   typhoon
tipify   typify
tirade
tirannical   tyrannical
tire
tiro/tyro
tissue
tit   teat
titel   title
tithe
titian
titillate
title
titmouse
titular
to (preposition,
  see too, two)
toad
toastmaster
tobacco
toboggan
tocsin (signal,
  see toxin)
tode   toad
toddy
toe (foot digit,
  see tow)
toehead   towhead
toga
together
toggle

tole (painted tin,
   see toll)
tolerable
tolerant
tolerate
toll (tax, see
   tole)

tollerable	tolerable

tomahawk

tomaine	ptomaine

tomato
tomb
tomfoolery

tommahawk	tomahawk

tomorrow

tonage	tonnage

tonal

toncil	tonsil
toncillectomy	tonsillectomy
toncillitis	tonsillitis

tongue
tonic
tonight
tonnage
tonsil
tonsillectomy
tonsillitis
tonsorial
too (also, see
   to, two)
tooth
toothache
topaz
tope (to drink,
   see taupe)

topic
topple
topsy-turvy
Torah

torchous	tortuous

toreador

torent	torrent
torential	torrential
torid	torrid

torment
tornado

tornament	tournament

torpedo
torpid
torpor
torque

Torrah	Torah
torreador	toreador

torrent
torrential
torrid
torsion
torso
tort (civil
   wrong)
torte (dessert)
tortilla
tortoise
tortuous
torture
total
totalitarian
totality
totem
touch
touche/touché

tough		trajectory	
tought	taught	trammeled	
toupee		trample	
tour de force		trampoline	
tourist		trance	
tournament		tranquil	
tourney		tranquilizer	
tourniquet		transact	
toushe	touche/	transatlantic/	
	touché	trans-Atlantic	
tow (cart, see		transcend	
toe)		transcendental	
toward		transcribe	
towel		transcription	
tower		transe	trance
towhead		transend	transcend
town		transendental	transcendental
toxic		transfer	
toxin (poison,		transference	
see tocsin)		transfiguration	
trace		transfixed	
trachea		transformation	
trachoma		transfusion	
tractable		transgress	
traction		transience	
tractor		transient	
tradition		transistor	
traffic		transition	
trafficker		transitional	
tragectory	trajectory	transitive	
tragedy		transitory	
tragic		translate	
trailer		translucent	
train		transmigration	
trait		transmit	
traitor		transmittal	

transmitter		treat	
transmute		treatise	
transom		treaty	
transparent		treble	
transpire		tred	tread
transplant		trefoil	
transport		trek	
transpose		trekked	
transposition		trellis	
transverse		tremble	
transvestite		tremendous	
tranzlucent	translucent	tremolo	
trapeze		tremor	
trapezoid		tremulous	
trapper		trenchant	
Trappist		trepidation	
trase	trace	trespasser	
trate	trait	tressel	trestle
trauma		trestle	
traumatic		trial	
travail		triangle	
travel		tribal	
travelogue		tribe	
traverse		tribulation	
travesty		tribune	
trawler		tributary	
treacherous		tribute	
treachery		triceps	
treacle		trichina	
treacly		trichinosis	
treadle		trickery	
treadmill		trickle	
treason		tricycle	
treasure		trident	
treasurer		triennial	

trifling
trigger
trilingual
trillion
trillium
trilogy
trimming
trinity
trinket
trio
tripartite
triple
triplet
triptych
triumph
triumvirate
trivet
trivia
trivial
troche (lozenge)
trochee (meter)
trodden
troff   trough
troglodyte
trojectory   trajectory
trolley
trollop
trombone
troop (soldiers,
  see troupe)
tropesphere   troposphere
trophy
tropic
tropism
troposphere

trotter
troubadour
trouble
trough
troul   trowel
troupe (per-
  formers, see
  troop)
trousers
trousseau
trout
trowel
truancy
truant
trubadour   troubadour
truce
truckage
truculence
trudge
true
truency   truancy
truent   truant
truffle
trumpeter
truncate
trundle bed
truso   trousseau
truss
trustee (adminis-
  trator, see
  trusty)
trustful
trustworthy
trusty (reliable,
  see trustee)

trysting		tushe	touche/touché
tsar/czar		tussle	
tsetse fly		tutelage	
tubercular		tutelary	
tuberculosis		Tutonic	Teutonic
tuberous		tutor	
tubular		toxedo	
tufted		twain	
tuition		tweak	
tularemia		tweed	
tumoltuous	tumultuous	tweeter	
tumor		tweezer	
tumultuous		twelfth	
tundra		twentieth	
tungsten		twenty	
tunic		tweter	tweeter
tunnel		twezer	tweezer
tupee	toupee	twich	twitch
turban		twilight	
turbine		twinge	
turbulent		twinkle	
tureen		twirl	
turgid		twitch	
turmoil		two (number,	
turn (rotate,		see to, too)	
see tern)		tycoon	
turnament	tournament	tyfoid	typhoid
turney	tourney	tyfoon	typhoon
turnip	tourniquet	tyfus	typhus
turniquet		tyke	
turnstile		tympany (bom-	
turpentine		bast, see	
turpitude		timpani)	
turquoise		typeographical	typograph-
turret			ical

typewriter	typographical
typhoid	typography
typhoon	tyrannical
typhus	tyranny
typical	tyrant
typify	tyro/tiro

U

ubiquitous
ucalyptus   eucalyptus
Ucharist   Eucharist
uchre   euchre
udder (gland,
   see utter)
udomoter
ufemism   euphemism
ufonic   euphonic
ugenic   eugenic
ugh
ukulele
ulcer
ulceration
ulcerous
ulogistic   eulogistic
ulogize   eulogize
ulogy   eulogy
ultamatum   ultimatum
ulterior
ultimate
ultimatum
ultraviolet
umber
umbilical cord

umbrage
umbrella
umlaut
umph   oomph
unabridged
unaccountable
unaccustomer
unaffected
unanimity
unanimous
unassuming
unavoidable
unbeknownst
unbiased
unbidden
unbridled
uncanny
unceremonious
uncertainty
uncivilized
uncle
uncomfortable
uncommitted
uncommon
uncommunicative

uncompromising	unharnessed
unconditional	unhurried
unconscionable	unicameral
unconscious	unicorn
unconstitutional	unification
uncouth	uniformity
unction	unify
unctuous	unilateral
undaunted	unimpeachable
undemonstrative	unique
undeniable	unison
undercurrent	unitary
undernourished	universal
undesirable	universe
undoubtedly	university
undulation	unkempt
unduly	unknowable
uneasiness	unleash
unemployable	unlimited
unequal	unmentionable
unequivocal	unmercifully
unerring	unmitigated
unexpurgated	unnatural
unfamiliarity	unnecessary
unfaned unfeigned	unnumbered
unfasten	unoccupied
unfeigned	unparalleled
unfettered	unplumbed
unflinching	unprecedented
unforgettable	unprejudiced
unfortunate	unprincipled
unfriendliness	unpronounceable
unfurled	unqualified
ungainliness	unquestionable
ungrateful	unraveled
unhappiness	unreality

unremitting		uphoria	euphoria
unrighteous		upward	
unrivaled		uranium	
unruffled		urban	
unsaturated		urbane	
unsavory		urchin	
unseasonable		ureka	eureka
unseemly		urethra	
unshackled		urgent	
unsheathe		urinal	
unsophisticated		urinary	
unsparing		urn	
unsuitable		urology	
untangled		usher	
untrammeled		ustachian tube	Eustachian tube
untutored		usurp	
unuch	eunuch	usury	
unusual		utensil	
unwanted		uterine	
unwarrantable		uterus	
unwary		uthanasia	euthanasia
unwholesome		utilitarian	
unwieldy		utility	
unwitting		utopian	
unwonted		utter (speak, see	
upheaval		udder)	
uphemism	euphuism	utterance	
upholstery		uvula	
uphonic	euphonic		

V

vabrato	vibrato	valence (weights, see valance)	
vacant		valentine	
vacation		valese	valise
vaccinate		valet	
vaccine		valiant	
vaccum	vacuum	valid	
vacillate		validity	
vacsinate	vaccinate	valise	
vacsine	vaccine	valley	
vacuity		valocity	velocity
vacuous		valor	
vacuum		valour	velour
vagabond		valuable	
vagary		valuminous	voluminous
vagina		valuptuous	voluptuous
vagrancy		vampire	
vague		vanacular	vernacular
vain (idle, see vane, vein)		vandal	
vainglorious		vane (weather-cock, see vain, vein)	
valance (drapery, see valence)			
vale (valley, see veil)		vaneer	veneer
valedictorian		vanguard	
		vanilla	

vanity		vellum	
vanquish		velocity	
vantage		velour	
vapid		velvet	
vapor		venal	
vaporous		venason	venison
variant		vender/vendor	
varicose vein		vendetta	
variegate		veneal	veniel
variety		veneer	
various		venerable	
varsity		venerate	
vary (change,		venereal	
see very)		vengeance	
vascular		vengeful	
vas deferens		venial	
vasectomy		venison	
vasomotor		venom	
vassal		venomous	
vassalage		venous	
vaudeville		ventilate	
vault		ventilator	
veal		ventral	
vecissitude	visissitude	ventriloquist	
vector		venture	
veer		venue	
vegetable		venum	venom
vegetarian		venus	venous
vegetate		veola	viola
vehement		veracious (truth,	
vehicle		see voracious)	
veil (screen, see		veracose vein	varicose vein
vale)		veranda	
vein (channel, see		verbal	
vain, vane)		verbatim	

verbena   vestal
verbiage   vestibule
verbose   vestige
verboten   vestigial
verdant   vetch
verdict   veteran
verdure   veterinary
verge   vexation
verify   vi   vie
verily   via
verisimilitude   viable
veritable   viaduct
verity   vial (cup, see
vermicelli   vile)
vermilion   vialable   violable
vermin   viand
vermouth   vibrate
vernacular   vibrato
vernal equinox   vibrator
verranda   veranda   vicar
versatile   vicarious
verse   vice (defect, see
versification   vise)
version   vice versa
versus   vichyssoise
vertebra   vicinity
vertebrate   vicious
vertex   vicissitude
vertical   victim
vertigo   victor
very (much,   victual
  see vary)   vicuna/vicuña
vesheswase   vichyssoise   video
vespers   vie
vessel   viend   viand

vigil		virtual	
vigilance		virtue	
vigilante		virtuosity	
vignette		virtuoso	
vigor		virtuous	
viament	vehement	virulence	
vile (foul, see		virus	
vial)		visa	
vilify		visage	
village		vis-a-vis/vis-à-vis	
villain (rogue)		visceral	
villein (serf)		viscose	
vinaigrette sauce		viscount	
vinal	vinyl	vise (tool, see	
vincible		vice)	
vindetta	vendetta	viseral	visceral
vindicate		visheswase	vichyssoise
vindictive		visible	
vinegar		vision	
vinegret sauce	vinaigrette	visitor	
	sauce	visor	
vineyard		vissage	visage
vintage		vista	
vinyet	vignette	visual	
vinyl		vitality	
viola		vitamin	
violable		vitiate	
violate		vitrefy	vitrify
violence		vitreous	
violet		vitrify	
violin		vitriol	
viper		vittal	victual
virago		vituperate	
virgin		vivacious	
virile		vivacity	

vivesection	vivisection	voluminous
vivid		voluntary
viviparous		volunteer
vivisection		voluptuous
vizier		voodoo
vizor	visor	voracious (engulf-
vocabulary		ing, see veracious)
vocalize		voracity
vociferous		vortex
vodka		vortical
vodville	vaudeville	votary
vogue		voucher
voice		vowel
voile		voyage
volatile		voyeur
volcano		vulcanize
volition		vulgar
Volkswagen		Vulgate
volley		vulnerable
volocity	velocity	vulture
voltage		vulva
voluble		vying
volume		

W

waddle

wafe waif

wafer

waffle

waft

wager

waggish

wagon

waif

wail (cry, see
 wale, whale)

wain (cart, see
 wane)

wainscot

waist (between
 chest and hips,
 see waste)

wait (postpone,
 see weight)

waive (forgo, see
 wave)

walaby wallaby

wale (texture,
 see wail, whale)

walet wallet

walkie-talkie

wallaby

wallet

walleyed pike

wallop

wallow

walnut

walrus

waltz

wammy whammy

wampum

wanderer

wane (decrease,
 see wain)

wangle

wanton

warbler

warden

wardrobe

ware (articles,
 see wear, where)

warehouse

warf wharf

warn

warrant

warranty

warrior

wary

wash

wassail

Wassermann test

waste (squander,
see waist)

wastrel

watt (electric,
see what)

wattle

wavering

wave (fluctuate,
see waive)

waxen

way (route, see
weigh, whey)

we (all of us, see
oui)

weak (feeble, see
week)

weal (welt, see
we'll, wheal,
wheel)

wealth

wean

weapon

wear (put on, see
ware, where)

wearisome

wearwolf   werewolf

weary

weasel

weather (climate,
see whether,
wether)

weave

weevil

webbing

wedding

wedge

Wedgie

Wedgwood ware

wedlock

wee   we (all of us)
             oui (yes)

weedle   wheedle

weege board   ouija board

week (time, see
weak)

ween   wean

weesel   weasel

weeve   weave

weevil

weigh (measure,
see way, whey)

weight (measure,
see wait)

weird

weld

welfare

we'll (we will, see
wheal, weal,
wheel)

welterweight

wence   whence

werewolf

wery   wary

westerner

westward

wether (ram, see
weather, whether)

whetstone

whale (mammal,
  see wail, wale)
whammy
wharf
what (pronoun,
  see watt)
wheal (welt, see
  weal, we'll,
  wheel)
wheat
wheedle
wheel (tire, see
  weal, we'll,
  wheal)
wheeze
whence
where (place,
  see ware, wear)
wherry
whether (con-
  junction, see
  weather,
  wether)
whetstone
whey (curds and,
  see way, weigh)
which (pronoun,
  see wich, witch)
whiff
Whig (political
  party, see wig)
while (conjunction,
  see wile)
whimper
whimple   wimple
whimsey

whimsical
whine (cry, see
  wine)
whinny
whiporwill   whippoorwill
whippersnapper
whippet
whippoorwill
whirl
whisk broom
whiskey/whisky
whisper
whist
whistle
whither (where
  to, see wither)
whittle
whiz
whoa
whole (all, see
  hole)
whoopee
whooping cough
whopper
whore (prostitute,
  see hoar)
whorl
who's (who is)
whose (possessive)
wich (tree, see
  which, witch)
wicked
wicker
wicket
widow
width

wield
wiff   whiff
wig (hair, see
  Whig)
wiggle
wigwam
wilderness
wile (trick,
  see while)
will-o'-the-wisp
willow
willy-nilly
wimple
wimper   whimper
wimsey   whimsey
wimsical   whimsical
wince
winch
window
wine (drink,
  see whine)
winnow
winsome
wiper
wippersnapper   whipper-
                                snapper
wipporwill   whippoorwill
wisdom
wiseacre
wiskbroom   whiskbroom
wist   whist
wistaria/wisteria
Wistershire sauce   Worcestershire
                                sauce

witch (woman,
  see which,
  wich)
witicism   witticism
wither (shrivel,
  see whither)
witness
witticism
wizard
wizen
wobble
woebegone
woeful
woffer   woofer
wolverine
womb
wombat
wonder
wondrous
wont (habit)
won't (will not)
woo
wood (lumber,
  see would)
woofer
wooppee   whooppee
Worcestershire
  sauce
world
worse
worship
worst (bad, see
  wurst)
worsted

Worstershire
  sauce

Worcester-
  shire sauce

would (past
  tense of will,
  see wood)
wound
wraith
wrangler
wrapped (cover,
  see rapped,
  rapt)
wrath
wreak (inflict,
  see reek)
wreath
wreathe
wreck
wren
wrench
wrest (distort,
  see rest)

wrestler
wretch (vile
  person, see
  retch)
wriggle
wright (play-
  wright, see right,
  rite, write)
wrinkle
wrist
writ
write (jot down,
  see right, rite,
  wright)
writhe
wrong
wrought
wry (bent, see
  rye)
wurst (meat,
  see worst)

X

xenophobia
Xerox
X-ray

xylocaine
xylophone

Y

yacht
yak
yawn
yearning
yeast
yellow
yeoman
yesterday
Yiddish
yield
yodel
yogurt/yoghurt

yogi
yoke (frame,
  see yolk)
yolk (egg, see
  yoke)
yoman
Yom Kuppur
your (possessive)
you're (you are)
yowl
yuletide

Z

zeal

zealot

zealous

zelot   zealot

zenith

zennia   zinnia

zenophobia   xenophobia

zephyr

zeppelin

zero

zinc

zinnia

zipper

zither

zodiac

zombi

zone

zoological

zoology

Zoroastrian

zucchini

zwieback

zygote

zylocaines   xylocaines

zylophone   xylophone